May 19/77
Toronto

Kindly Bent to Ease Us

Klong-chen rab-'byams-pa

Part Two: Meditation
bSam-gtan ngal-gso

from

The Trilogy of Finding Comfort and Ease
Ngal-gso skor-gsum

Translated from the Tibetan and annotated by

Herbert V. Guenther

DHARMA PUBLISHING

TIBETAN TRANSLATION SERIES

Calm and Clear
The Legend of the Great Stupa
Mind in Buddhist Psychology
Golden Zephyr
Kindly Bent to Ease Us, Part One
Kindly Bent to Ease Us, Part Two
Kindly Bent to Ease Us, Part Three

Illustrations:
Frontispiece: Kun-tu-bZang-po (Samantabhadra),
the Adi or primordial Buddha
Page 40: Klong-chen rab-'byams-pa
Page 52: Rahula, an important Nyingma Dharma Protector
Page 91: Stūpa, a symbol of the Mind of the Buddha

ISBN: 0-913546-42-9; 0-913546-43-7 (pbk)
Library of Congress Number: 75-29959

Typeset in Fototronic Elegante and printed by
Dharma Press, Emeryville, California
9 8 7 6 5 4 3 2 1

To Tarthang Tulku Rinpoche

Contents

Foreword

This second volume of Longchenpa's *Trilogy* focuses on the specific practice of Dzogchen meditation. Traditionally, such a text is meant to be an outline or synthesis of an enormous depth of teachings which are difficult to express verbally or conceptually. These teachings, therefore, are not ordinarily practiced without an explanation of the words and symbols by a teacher in the 'lineage', and only after thorough study does a person receive additional instruction and guidance in the meaning and application of the text. This oral instruction is essential because it 'completes' or 'finishes' the text and properly initiates the student into its practice. Therefore, it is very important for the person to listen to the instruction carefully, to think about what he has read or heard, and then to realize the teaching through his life.

Texts of this nature have three levels of explanation —outer, inner, and secret. The first level is the direct or literal interpretation of the text called *lung*; second, the word-for-word commentary of specific meanings and connotations called *khrid*; and third, the initiations, or *dbang*. The *lung*, or texts, explain the correct procedure for performing the practices and guide the individual through the proper patterns of development—how to visualize the mandala or perform the sadhana, and how to work with difficulties encountered within the practice. This initial, theoretical preparation is followed by *khrid* in which the teacher may give the student certain exercises or specific 'tests' to see how much he understands and how far he can proceed with the practice in his own experience, and to determine whether or not the student is ready to receive further instruction. If the 'test' is successful, then certain oral teachings may be given in a more direct manner. There are also many different kinds of *dbang* or initiations—various explanations, symbolic expressions, gestures, and visions through which the meaning of the teaching is directly and inwardly realized.

Each text, therefore, contains a map, or specific instructions for becoming enlightened. But first, at the preliminary, psychological level, it is very important to clean up mental or emotional blockages and to prepare the soil for the understanding to grow. Basically, as human beings, we have many different intellectual and emotional patterns, and we become 'fixed' in certain ways of seeing and behaving. The Vajrayana has many methods to liberate karmic obscurations—not necessarily through analysis or investigation, suppression or confrontation, but through certain inner 'initiations' or 'cleansings'. Without this cleansing of our psychological confusions, it is not possible to understand the deeper, more hidden teachings.

The main purpose of all Buddhist teaching is to experience its truth for ourselves—to see clearly and to directly contact our own inner understanding. So it is possible that a person who is seriously practicing one text or one meditation can achieve Enlightenment. But commonly, human interpretations are very limited, and certain kinds of knowledge or inner experience are difficult to understand without guid-

ance. Like the sun and its rays, the thread or key to Enlightenment is continuously being transmitted through the
inner guidance of the living lineage. So the person who
follows these instructions—beyond verbal explanations and
symbols—can completely trust them until he realizes the
teachings within his own awareness. This is how the 'lineage
of direct realization'—or the Nyingma Dzogchen lineage as
represented by Longchenpa—has continued to survive for
many centuries.

For many Westerners, the Buddhist tradition may often
seem complex and difficult. Everyone would like the teachings to be explained very simply. But, while words and
concepts can be useful, they are not sufficient. As with a good
meal, we eat and walk away satisfied, but soon we are hungry
again. So certain teachings may seem complicated unless we
are ready to hear them on a more inward level. That is why
the Nyingma tradition has always emphasized study and
practice together. Once we become more familiar with
Buddhist concepts, we realize that intellectual explanations
and philosophical theories originate in direct experience. So
read these words by Longchenpa very carefully and think
about them. Each word and image seems very important.

Once again, I am deeply grateful to Dr. Guenther for
continuing his efforts to present this important knowledge to
Western readers. Even Tibetans may feel that this text is
extremely difficult to translate because it is based on very
deep meditative insight. However, I personally feel that the
heart of Longchenpa's message is quite clear, and that anyone who reads this translation will find something of great
value for his life.

The Tibetan tradition has many excellent and beautiful
texts. In five or six years we have tried to make a few publi-
cations available through Dharma Press, and in the future, as
more students learn Tibetan, we hope to present many more
volumes and to extend the teachings of Buddhism and the

Nyingma lineage to anyone interested in developing his own potential. By the merit of these positive actions, may Long-chenpa's teaching and Padmasambhava's blessing help sentient beings everywhere to overcome frustration and wake up to Enlightenment.

Sarvam Mangalam

Nyingma Institute   TARTHANG TULKU RINPOCHE
Berkeley, California

Preface

In recent years meditation has gained considerable publicity. The inevitable result of the accompanying propaganda has furthered a widely held belief that any, if not a particular, brand will 'do the trick' irrespective of the person who uses it. Klong-chen rab-'byams-pa's dissertation on this controversial subject comes as a timely corrective because he re-instates the centrality of *man*, on whom everything depends. He does not prejudge man, but sees each individual involved in a process of growth, a process which does not take place in isolation or a vacuum, but in an environment which creates and molds man as much as it is man's creation. Since whatever man does has wider implications, it must be permeated by a sense of direction which ultimately is rooted in the knowledge of 'where' he is going and of 'what' he is becoming, which is merely the manifest expression of this knowledge.

'Meditation', for Klong-chen rab-'byams-pa, is thus not an end in itself, but a unique device for tuning in to a reality which man is constantly—actively and creatively—shaping.

Any device has the tendency to become an end in itself, but, seen as something dynamic, it furthers understanding and action to aid us in orienting ourselves and providing us with insight and direction. The moment we take a step in a certain direction we have already gone beyond ourselves so that we are no longer some static, pre-defined essence, but are participating in an evolutionary process of growth which leads to further, greater, and wider complexities. What may have been exclusively valid on one level loses its exclusiveness on the next higher one, and is superseded by a higher-order comprehensiveness; if this were not the case there would be no growth but mere stagnation.

For this very reason Klong-chen rab-'byams-pa is very critical of facile 'cure-all' prescriptions. What he wants us to do is to take the 'big jump' that sets us free from a preoccupation with mere 'techniques' and other props which are the stock and trade of the person of 'low intelligence', who is particularly prone to aberrations and excesses. In order to grow, to be able to take the 'big jump', we must look forward and learn to tune in to what, from one viewpoint, lies ahead and, from another, emanates from a higher level. In this phase of our being, 'imagination', as the ability to devise fresh models for the disclosure of the meaningfulness of an ultimately 'intelligent' universe, is of paramount importance, although it must not be used as an end in itself.

As in part one of the *Trilogy*, Klong-chen rab-'byams-pa has structured each chapter in this work in a distinct manner. In indicating this structure I have followed the same principle as in the first part, but have simplified the very intricate pattern of the third chapter in accordance with Klong-chen rab-'byams-pa's commentary. His own structural analysis in the *rDzogs-pa chen-po bSam-gtan ngal-gso'i bsdus-don Puṇḍa-rīka'i phreng-ba* makes almost every line a topic in itself.

Because of the highly technical nature of this dissertation, I have used Klong-chen rab-'byams-pa's other writings extensively in order to give the Western reader some insight into the depth and scope of rNying-ma thought. Here, as in so many other cases, I gratefully acknowledge the help given me by my friend Tarthang Tulku who has always been concerned with having the wealth of rNying-ma thought and its application in life available to a larger audience.

I am grateful to my colleagues and friends, professors Keith Scott and Leslie Sumio Kawamura, and Mr. Steven D. Goodman and Mr. Stephen Tainer, for critical comments; and above all, to my wife for her sustained interest and unflagging patience in preparing the final form of the manuscript.

Finally, I have to thank the editorial staff of Dharma Publishing for their careful work on the typescript, Miss Judy Robertson for designs, Mr. Kennard Lipman for his assistance in proofreading, and Mr. Paul Clemens for the preparation of the index.

Anniversary of   HERBERT V. GUENTHER
Klong-chen rab-'byams-pa's
Parinirvāṇa,
February 16, 1976
Saskatoon/Berkeley

Kindly Bent to Ease Us

Introduction

The second part of Klong-chen rab-'byams-pa's *Trilogy of Finding Comfort and Ease* is the shortest and most technical, and yet in its conciseness, which at first glance may seem enigmatic, it contains a wealth of observation and information not readily accessible elsewhere. Its theme is 'meditation' (*bsam-gtan*) in its specific rDzogs-chen connotation. The English term 'meditation' has been much abused in modern usage, commercially and otherwise, yet its original and basic ambiguity, apart from the noticeable abuse and misuse, still has a certain heuristic value. In its transitive use it implies a definite directing or focussing of thought and, in this sense, it approximates the ideas of intending and purposing. It also connotes persistent concentration of attention. In its intransitive use it suggests an effort to understand a thing in all its aspects, values, and relationships, but even in this sense, the transitive application reverberates in its intransitive one.

The Tibetan term *bsam-gtan* corresponds, to a certain extent, to the transitive use of the English word 'meditation', particularly because it constitutes an aspect of what is to become the noetic-noematic complex (*sems*), usually rendered by 'mind' or, more actively, 'mentation' and referring to the process of consciousness dealing with a specific object. Its most generic feature is that it is 'intentive' to objects, that is, objects are eventually 'intended by' the process of consciousness, which we associate with a 'subject', a reflective ego. Inasmuch as these 'objects' to be intended by consciousness have a certain meaning for and through consciousness, they point to certain sets of modes of consciousness (as process) which have these specific objects as their correlates. The term *bsam-gtan* applies to this 'setting' of an as yet preconscious intending, which gradually becomes frozen into the customary subject-object division, on any level where the noetic-noematic correlation is in its formation.

Inasmuch as emphasis here tends to be laid on what is to become the reflective-thematic aspect of experience, more and more engrossed with explicit reflective discrimination, this 'setting' is already a kind of limitation of the open dimension of Being. In terms of cognition, this open dimension of Being is 'pure awareness' (*rig-pa*) which, in itself, as the ever-present pre-reflective non-thematic aspect of experience, remains a free 'bestowing of sense', Buddhahood intentionality (*dgongs-pa*).[1] *bsam-gtan* and *dgongs-pa*, although distinct from each other, indicate structural directions and deployments within experience. To be more precise, *bsam-gtan* characterizes the moment of transition when the latent discriminating determinations, that become an explicating and concentrating attention, begin stirring and are going to move freely in the context of explicit themes such as subject and object, whereby they harden into 'mind' (*sems*). This particular transitional moment within experience is termed the 'spontaneous' or 'self-present' or 'natural' setting. In picturesque language Klong-chen rab-'byams-pa declares:[2]

Here, in this palace adorned by a display of spontaneous
    richness,
The king, self-existing pristine cognitiveness, sits on his
    throne.
While all the creative impulses of pristine cognitiveness,
    present as the coming and going (of thought),
Have become ministers and govern the country,
The noble queen, a self-present setting, and
Their son with his servants, self-manifested Buddha
    intentionality,
Have gathered in the midst of pure pleasure, radiant in
    themselves, without dividing thoughts.

He elaborates on this verse as follows:[3]

Here, self-existent, spontaneous pure awareness is the layout
of a palace; in it all meanings are complete inasmuch as
'founding strata of meaning' and 'founded pristine cognitions
of meaning' are such that they cannot be added to nor
subtracted from each other. As is stated in the *Yi-ge med-pa*:[4]

Since in me there is neither without nor within,
Lucency is perfectly complete;
Since in me there is neither no-thing-ness
    nor some-thing-ness,
Presence is perfectly complete.

Thus, the very facticity of the spontaneously present vitalizing power of Being is self-existent pristine cognitiveness, like
a king who does not leave his throne. The self-present actual
setting within this facticity is like the queen, because it has
never been experienced apart from pure awareness. The
warmth of Buddha intentionality, that is there in its own
right, once one has understood what is meant, is like the
prince and his servants. The cognitive capacity that goes out
to its objects, a self-creative movement that comes from the
reach and range of pure awareness, is like the ministers who
govern the country and provide the necessities.

If one does not make this distinction one would be no
different from a drunken person talking nonsense. Hence one

must know that, within self-existent pristine cognitiveness that has been and will be forever, self-present and spontaneous facticity is independent of (any) object, and that the pristine cognitiveness—which, as a creative movement performing the act of cognition, emerges in the direction of an object—depends on the object. Since there is a great difference between the conditions that lead to a state of dividedness if one is not aware of the (original) relaxed state and that which is there in itself, it is by recognizing the self-existent (character of pristine cognitiveness) within, that its creative movement becomes free in and on its (very) ground. This is said to be the reach and range of primordial purity where all (contrived) meaning has ceased.

Since the creative movement with its divisiveness enters the object by (going away from) the indeterminate aspect of the self-existent (pristine cognitiveness)—if the latter is not recognized for what it is—it is important to recognize the Buddha intentionality that does not admit of any break, together with the actual (self-present) setting. Facticity and specification are discussed in the *Kun-byed*[5] as follows:

> Listen, O great being:
> Pristine cognitiveness which is called pristine
>   cognitiveness
> Is cognitiveness since all beginning;
> It is self-existent, cognitive since all beginning.
> The pristine cognitiveness that conceives of an object
> Derives from the object and is not self-existent;
> In the mere absence of an object it is not illumining.
> Therefore, the self-existent pristine cognitiveness
> Is a pristine cognitiveness that is cognitive since all
>   beginning.
> This is what is meant by pristine cognitiveness.
> The pristine cognitiveness that is the teacher of the
>   entourage
> Is a pristine cognitiveness that discriminates between
>   objects.
> This discriminating between objects

Is a pristine cognitiveness that performs the act of
    cognizing,
Because the object that is being cognized
Derives from the mind in limpid clearness and
    consummate perspicacity.
This mind in limpid clearness and consummate
    perspicacity in which no object obtains
Derives from pristine cognitiveness itself, hence
There is no imaginative activity with holistic
    experiences.
Tendencies towards holistic experiences are not
    engendered.
This very meaningfulness in which no tendencies are
    present
Is said to be the intentionality of all the Buddhas of the
    three times.
The intentionality of all the Buddhas of the three times
Is not divided as to objective (content).
It has remained the same since beginningless time.

Within this self-existent pristine cognitiveness that is not
divided as to objective contents, the very spontaneity, un-
contrived, of the self-present setting is the meditative setting
for those who tune themselves in to a higher reality, while
inner calm and wider perspective that focus the (ego-bound)
mind on an object are the (meditative) setting for worldly
simpletons. The difference lies between building up or not
building up tendencies. The self-present fact of pure awareness, which is mind in limpid clearness and consummate
perspicacity, is termed 'meaningfulness-(directed) intentionality'. The cognitive capacity that rises in the direction of
objects is termed 'samsaric mind'; it is born in the form of
noetic (grasping) and noematic (content). Furthermore, when
there is the cognitiveness of relaxation in the reach and range
(of self-existent pristine cognitiveness) after it has been
recognized for what it is, the creative movement of the self-
existent cognitiveness subsides in its very ground, and intentionality becomes pure meaningfulness. Since these two
ideas are quite different, the *Kun-byed*[6] again says:

> Listen, O great being:
> In the spirituality which is the self-existent pristine
>   cognitiveness
> Of all the Buddhas of the three times,
> There has, since the very beginning, never been any
>   dividedness.
> This cognitiveness as such does not enact Buddha
>   intentionality.
> It is separate from any object (belonging to) dividedness.
> If any person who tunes in to a higher reality in any way
> Changes over to a state where no dividedness obtains,
> He enacts Buddha intentionality.
> Since self-existing pristine cognitiveness is not divided
>   as to objective (content),
> It is not shrouded in the tendencies towards
>   dividedness.

The upshot of this lengthy discussion is that both *bsam-gtan* and *dgongs-pa* constitute an existential cross-section, both interpenetrating in such a manner that two directions can be followed. In one case, the movement is in the direction of reflective discrimination, though it is not reflective discrimination itself; in the other case, the movement will not be disturbed by reflective discrimination. Nonetheless, both movements are tendential in character: the one (*bsam-gtan*) is orientated towards thematic concerns, the other (*dgongs-pa*) towards a non-thematic range that conveys immediate felt meanings tied up with a totality field. At the same time a hierarchical order is implied—*dgongs-pa* encompasses *bsam-gtan*, not the other way round.

As a 'setting', *bsam-gtan* is built into the psychophysical organization of the human individual and, specifically, points to the contemporaneity of a prereflective self-referentiality, which becomes noticeable in the birth of a decision or the execution of an action, with the project or action to be embarked upon. The prereflective self-referentiality is pointed out in Klong-chen rab-'byams-pa's statement that[7]

(This natural setting) may suddenly stir and be aroused from its mere thereness in all living beings when the cognitive capacity begins to vibrate in its dormancy. It is that which exists in the eyes of an arrow straightener, in the eyes of a hare and a hawk resting in its nest, and so on. In brief, it exists whenever consciousness is roused from its dormancy.

It is then, with the conscious execution of a project, that the ego (or self) develops in such a way that it remains within, and 'inhabits', as it were, the action. It is never prior to the action; it discovers itself in it. In other words, *bsam-gtan* is something like a symbiosis of actor and action. The important point to note in all these instances is that the 'agent' or person who 'meditates' is an integral factor in this process. The agent apprehends (and enacts) his intentions in definite perspectives (*sems*) which are his finitudes. At the same time, however, any such finitude is an openness (*byang-chub sems*), and the agent, therefore, is not riveted to only one specific perspective or situation. The agent is able to appreciate perspectives other than the one he is deploying at a given moment. In view of the fact that the agent is an integral factor within the ongoing process, it is significant that *bsam-gtan* is said to be characteristic of 'ethical man' (Bodhisattva, *byang-chub sems-dpa'*) because he is one whose mind (*sems*) can, and is about to, become open to limpid clearness and consummate perspicacity (*byang-chub*) whose resonance (*dpa'*) shows itself in 'ethical man's' mind (*sems*). It is basically a mere continuation and variation of this 'setting' when it is said to be operative in those who have reached the various spiritual levels.[8]

However, 'ethical man' whose 'setting' is marked by being a more coherent (equilibrium) structure which can serve as a stable basis for later processes—it can 'lead on' and, hence, is unlikely to 'peter out'—is only a step in the evolutionary[9] movement as exemplified by man. Three such evolutionary phases can be distinguished. The lowest level is the one represented by 'gods and human beings', gods being analogues to human beings, a great deal more powerful, but not necessarily morally superior. The next higher phase is that of 'ethical man' who has risen above the crowd and above the mass individual (who is torn and divided by passing whims). 'Ethical man' is concerned with norms which make a person tune in with a life-stream, and the highest or optimal phase is the one of Buddha intentionality. Each of these phases involves a kind of insight which is then pursued as the purpose in and of life through the exercise of creative imagination. Thus, in the *Nyi-ma dang zla-ba kha-sbyor-ba chen-po gsang-ba'i rgyud*,[10] we read:

> Pursuit of life's meaning is threefold: (purposive) concentrating of mind as is done among gods (and men); the (coordinate) setting in Mahāyāna; and the intentionality of all the Buddhas throughout the three aspects of time.

Similarly the *Rig-pa rang-shar chen-po'i rgyud*[11] declares:

> Pursuit of life's meaning is pointed out to have three (phases):
> It is claimed to be concentrating mind (*sems-'dzin*) as done by gods and men;
> The (coordinate) setting of ethical man (*byang-chub sems-dpa'i bsam-gtan*);
> And Buddha intentionality (*de-bzhin-gshegs-pa'i dgongs-pa*).

The same text also makes it quite clear that the 'setting' of ethical man is not a preoccupation with mind which—on the previous level is taken to be one entity among others and through whose cultivation a state of non-dividedness is temporarily achieved—remains one among many other entities in a basically dualistic mind-body separation. Rather, the non-dividedness of the 'setting' is spontaneous as it is embedded in and emerges out of the evolutionary stream, a stream not admitting of any dividedness in itself. But still, while on the lowest level we may deal with mind as an object in a detached way, and on the level of ethical man by being more deeply involved and more firmly rooted in non-dividedness, both levels are stratifications within the evolutionary process as a whole, which at its peak is likened to the open expanse of the sky. The hierarchical relationship in terms of 'non-dividedness' is such that the level of 'gods and men' is encompassed by that of the 'setting' of ethical man, which, in turn, is encompassed by Buddha intentionality. Hence, as the *Rig-pa rang-shar chen-po'i rgyud*[12] states, the lower level cannot bring forward, or set forth, or reveal the higher level although the higher one can do so with the lower ones by giving increased meaning and order (non-dividedness, non-randomness) to them.

In the light of this interpenetrating hierarchical order, differences in procedures (rather than in states) become similarities of increasing complexities. We must never forget that man's life is not something static but a continuous movement towards higher, more complex, more-informed universes of meaning acted out by the human individual, not so much by anticipating and straightforwardly realizing them, but by letting the higher levels define themselves. Maybe, only on the lower level—'gods and men'—is there control by mind of mind and body. On this level the person conceives of himself as having a body and a mind. He then feels that something has to be done about the situation in which he finds himself and therefore attempts to concentrate, but his concentration is *on* something or other, be it on the sensory objects or on an idea. Thus, one of the most important and helpful aids to concentration is deep breathing which prevents mind from wandering, at the same time making the person aware of the forces within him, flowing smoothly and pulsating rhythmically, but also charging him so that he 'glows' with vitality. Gradually a mental situation, such as a pure sensation of colors, sounds, and so on, develops, which may be termed an objective non-referential situation, that is, one having no epistemological object. Thus there are three major phases:

1. steadying the mind,
2. disengaging it from its beliefs in (and identification with) concrete entities, and
3. pure sensation.[13]

But, as the *Rig-pa rang-shar chen-po'i rgyud*[14] clearly states, this concentration is but a temporary phase and has little to do with the overall or finalistic approach: It remains, despite its being an 'objective' situation, a 'subjective' affair.

> This concentration of mind by mind as practiced by gods and men
> Is such that, when breathing by mouth and nose has been regulated,
> The subjective mind, no longer moving to and fro, there being no divisive forces,
> Is the cognitive capacity having become focussed.
> This is declared to be a temporary non-referential situation.
> It cannot reveal what is the ultimately real point.

Restating this rather technical presentation in simple language we may say that in being concerned with a temporarily induced state of pure sensation we miss out on the larger issue of life and growth.

To a certain extent the same situation applies to the next higher level, the 'setting' of ethical man who quite literally is ahead of ordinary men and their analogues. The 'setting' is there before the dichotomic mind (the noetic-noematic complex, *sems*) dissolves the unity and is caught in its dividedness. Therefore, this 'setting' cannot be controlled or commanded by the lower level 'mind', which, because of its generally dissociative character, is unable to hold a complex pattern of thought stable. It is this 'setting'—by virtue of being a higher-level organization and having a greater capability of providing stability as a basis for further complex processes to take place—that is able to do what 'mind' cannot do. Still, this 'setting' is of a low hierarchical order, although higher than the level of 'men and gods', and because of this fact it is not the final stage. Thus, the *Rig-pa rang-shar chen-po'i rgyud*[15] declares:

> Ethical man's setting
> Is not some concentrative controlling by the mind.
> It comes naturally or spontaneously.
> When one avails oneself of it, a dynamic wholeness is
>   evolved.
> Also, thoughts about food are dismissed.[16]
> It is deployed by those on the higher spiritual levels.
> Naturally there is no divisive referentiality.
> But even this setting is unable to reveal what is the
>   ultimately real point.

For, as Klong-chen rab-'byams-pa explains, the real issue is the overarching 'pure awareness' (*rig-pa*), sheer lucency (*'od-gsal*), not just a mere non-referential situation.

Although both levels are alike in being inadequate, while they are different in status insofar as the 'lower' one is temporarily induced and the 'higher' one is a more or less stable and permanent setting, what they again have in common is a non-reflective (non-dissociative, non-divided, non-interfering) attitude. Precisely through such an attitude, access to the life-stream's own origin is made possible, and the unity with the wholeness of meaningfulness is reestablished. It is tempting to speak of it as an 'inner' way, but actually it points beyond a 'within' and a 'without' towards something deeper which we cannot, without lessening its significance, label in any way. Because of this feature, our ordinary concepts, geared to a discriminatory state of affairs, are inadequate, if not misleading, and can be used only with the greatest caution.

The access to the life-stream opened up by the non-reflective, non-dissociative attitude is referred to by such terms as 'control centers' (*'khor-lo*) and 'conductors' (*rtsa*), which themselves are features, rather than separable parts, of a larger 'field' that is dynamic through and through. This is borne out by such statements as

> Where there are 'conductors' there also is 'motility', and wherever 'motility' extends there also extends the 'bioenergetic input'. The latter is twofold: 'bioenergetic input triggering morphogenesis' and 'bioenergetic input remaining the energizing force'.[17]

And,

> The basis of the living body is the triad of 'conductors', 'motility' and 'bioenergetic input'. Both 'conductors' and 'motility' fall under 'bioenergetic input'. 'The bioenergetic input that triggers morphogenesis' is the radiative energy (spectral frequency) of the four 'elemental forces'. They are the site for 'pure awareness'. (All of this) is indivisibly present.[18]

And,

> Although the body as a force field is shown to have this triad of 'conductors', 'motility' and 'bioenergetic input', actually it is not found as something different from the pure fact that is the one pristine cognitiveness.[19]

Our living body, our concrete existence, is a total field that is both derived and primary, and inasmuch as the 'conductors' and 'control centers' are found in the immediacy of the awareness and realization of the dynamic character of the life process, they put the focus back within. We can understand these 'control centers' and 'conductors' (or, to avoid any static misconceptions, 'flow-patterns') as indicating complex spatio-temporal configurations or structures together with regular arrays of substructures, setting up and being set up by circuits. They are thus the expression of an orderly process, and each stage or phase in this process is something like a cross-section through a spatio-temporal pattern. Whether we see this configuration as structure or as process, it remains physical and psychic at the same time—physical in the sense that it can be 'observed' and psychic in its being 'lived'. A further significant feature of this spatio-temporal configuration is its symmetry which is radial in the 'control centers' and bilateral in the 'conductors', the latter exhibiting right-handed and left-handed twists. Since right and left are reversed in what is to become a 'female' organism, psychological and physiological differences are functionally determined. Both right and left have significance for and aid cephalization whereby the central axis is polarized into an anterior and a posterior end with a growing emphasis on the 'head'.

There are four 'control centers'[20] of varying radial complexity, which emerge against the background of an utter openness—the open dimension of Being (in philosophical terms) or the immensity of space, the vastness of the clear sky (in sensuous terms)—which nevertheless reaches into the ordered whole presented by a human organism. Klong-chen rab-'byams-pa says of these four 'control centers' in a summary fashion:

> Thus, there come from among the four control centers first the 'navel', because it sets up the overall foundation of the body and what goes with it; then comes the 'heart', the memory storage, because the cognitive capacity ('intelligence') has set in; then comes the 'throat', the nutriment, because the relishing of the flavor of the cognitive processes is verbalized; and last comes the 'head', the top ordering capacity for the whole.[21]

Accordingly, when his elaboration of this process is presented in concise form, the first 'control center' to develop is termed 'initial generator control center' (*skyed-byed dang-po'i 'khor-lo*), because it initiates the programming of the manifold actions and emerging functions of the living organism in such a way that it will reach the form and functioning characteristic for the organism, be this, in the case of a human being, either a man or a woman. In the development of this 'control center' the process of synthesis (*chu*, 'water', 'cohesion') is primary. It is 'located' in the 'navel' (*lte*), which is the 'center' of the process in the sense that it becomes centered in itself and, by virtue of being a process, 'centers' itself between adjacent levels.

The next 'control center' in ascending order is termed 'memory storage control center' (*dran-pa 'dus-pa'i 'khor-lo*). It is marked by the primacy of gravitational forces (*sa* 'earth', 'solidification') which are necessary to prevent the escape of what may be said to include all that we have learned in the struggle for survival, and to retain this 'knowledge'. It marks the beginning of 'intelligence' (*shes-pa*). Therefore, it also plays a significant role in the duration of the organism's life. It is 'located' in the 'heart' (*snying-ga*), which is the 'center' for all that we have split into mind and emotions. In splitting these we have made them quite inadequate as a means of dealing with our self-imposed problems.

The third 'control center' to emerge is called 'nutrition storage focal point' (*ro-rnams 'dus-pa'i 'khor-lo*), in which metabolic processes (*me*, 'fire', 'combustion', 'temperature', 'heat') are predominant. It is 'located' in the 'throat' (*mgrin*), which can easily be associated with the monitoring agency in the process, and thus is significant for the organism's well-being, health, and capacity for enjoyment and intercommunication (*longs-spyod*), involving the internal as well as the external environment.

Lastly, topping all these 'control centers' is the 'top ordering system control center' (*rtse-mo rnam-par bkod-pa'i 'khor-lo*), which is 'located' in the head (*spyi-bo*), the 'top' in a living organism, bearing the eyes and other sensory organs. In this ordering, 'speed' is of primary importance, and hence it is related to 'motility' (*rlung*) which is needed to maintain the complexity of the whole 'system' which, in turn, requires 'motility' for efficient working, in particular, for working out the details for which the 'system' has been programmed. This 'control center', therefore, is active in the clarity (but also in the deficiency performance of the whole process if it is somehow misdeveloping) of the sensory capacities and in man's becoming 'kindness-endowed', that is, a Buddha.

When it has been said that in each of these 'control centers' one 'elemental force' is primary, this does not mean that the others are absent—they are merely functionally recessive in what may be termed an interlocking 'directorate'. There is another set of terms for these 'control centers' which complements and somewhat specifies related features. These are, in the same ascending order and in the same location, the 'control center of morphogenesis' (*sprul-pa'i 'khor-lo*), the 'control center of meaning' (*chos-kyi 'khor-lo*), the 'control center of intercommunication' (*longs-spyod-kyi 'khor-lo*), and the 'control center of pure pleasure' (*bde-chen-gyi 'khor-lo*)[22]. The last-named center points, on the one hand, to the optimum performance of the process as a whole and, on the other, inseparable from it, to the optimum nature this process has when 'lived' by the individual in the course of knowing his own norms and capabilities. In this context, what has been seen as the emergence of 'intelligence' with its 'memory storage' here reiterates the point that our immediate sense-impressions, as well as our thought-processes, drawn from perception and memory, tend to be complex wholes and as such are 'meanings'. This movement towards ever increasing complexity can be diagrammed as in Figure 1 (p. 18).

The directionality in the morphogenesis of living organisms, termed 'cephalization', implies that this process is intrinsically 'intelligent'. The intrinsic intelligence of this process suggests that there are 'eyes' which 'see' (regulate) the direction of developmental movement. This process, discussed above, is an interaction between 'elemental forces' (*'byung-ba*) whose behavior is governed by their specific properties (termed synthesis, gravitation, and so on) tending towards 'condensation' (*snyigs-ma*)—similar to the chemical processes of polymerization and macromolecular formation

FIGURE 1

I	II	III
motility (*rlung*)	head (*spyi-bo*)	optimum ordering system (pure pleasure) (*bde-chen-gyi 'khor-lo*)
metabolism (*me*)	throat (*mgrin*)	intercommunication (monitoring) (*longs-spyod-kyi 'khor-lo*)
gravity (*sa*)	heart (*snying-ga*)	memory storage (meaning) (*chos-kyi 'khor-lo*)
synthesis (*chu*)	navel (*lte*)	morphogenesis (*sprul-pa'i 'khor-lo*)

————— pervasive medium of 'space' (*nam-mkha'*) —————

COLUMN I: the operationally dominant 'elemental force' (*byung-ba*) emergent within the 'pervasive medium of space' (*nam-mkha'*), which is also the 'openness of Being'.

COLUMN II: the 'localization' of the emergent elemental forces.

COLUMN III: the 'control centers' (*'khor-lo*)

↑   :   direction of arrows indicate ever-increasing complexity; this complexity develops within the pervasive medium of 'space'.

—and leading to the development of organic matter and the body-mind phenomenon. In another process, the 'internal radiation energy' (*dvangs-ma*) of the elemental forces leads to 'spiritual' operations. It is as if this latter concurrent process were 'looking into' the former process in a deeper and farther manner.

When the body is first begotten, there originate, first of all, within the complex of the 'initial generator' which has started from synthesis, the 'eyes of the lamps' and the 'eyes of the elemental forces'. How, (taking its direction) from the 'eyes of the elemental forces', the body, (being the interaction of) four elemental forces, is formed has been explained above. (Taking its direction) from the 'eyes of the lamps', there originate as the foundation for the presence of pristine cognition, for Nirvāṇa which actually and truly is lucency, bioenergetic cognitiveness, the founding stratum (for existential meanings), two wide-open extremities within the buffalo-horn-like conductors inside the orbs of the pupils of the eyes—these are the 'lamps that penetrate what they have seen in the far distance and drawn to themselves' (*rgyang-zhags chu'i sgron-ma*).[23]

It must not be assumed that, because of the reference to two sets of eyes, a dualistic principle is in any way involved; 'condensation' and 'radiation energy' are different perspectives of one and the same 'force'; in one case we 'see' dimly, in another we can 'see' clearly. Consequently, Saṃsāra and Nirvāṇa are 'perspectives' issuing from and converging in the living individual, yet never owned by him.

While the 'control centers', with their intricate network of 'conductors' and the 'circuits' set up by them, represent a hierarchical order of horizontal layers, radiating in all directions by virtue of their radial symmetry, the bilateral symmetry vitalizing and even organizing these 'control centers' and their networks is indicated by a triad of 'conductors'. These conductors, as 'circuits', are responsible for the differentiation into right and left, male and female, body and mind, not so much as irreconcilable opposites but as complementary, interacting facets of an all-pervading flow of life, a 'standing-wave pattern' that can be seen from without or within or from still another deeper/higher level:

> Thus, since the triad of *ro-ma*, *rkyang-ma*, and *kun-'dar-ma*, the vitalizing axle in the 'conductors' of the four 'control centers'

in the live body, outwardly sets up the triad of body, speech, and (ego)mind; inwardly the triad of existentiality, communication, and spirituality; and mystically the triad of the founding strata of meaning which become embodied as concrete bearers of meaning, of world horizons, and of meaning in an ultimate sense; this triad stands there straight like pillars.[24]

Although the illustration of this triad by 'pillars' seems to point to something approaching a solid entity or a rigid structure in which processes are somehow subordinate, actually it is the other way round: processes come first and structure is and remains more or less fluid. This is borne out by the definition of the three 'conductors' and by the fact that they are seen in the context of starting-point $\longrightarrow$ path (process) $\longrightarrow$ goal, where the 'starting-point' itself already presents a tension between the opposites of what is conventionally accepted to be the case and quite real operationally (*kun-rdzob*), and what really is the case and primary (*don-dam*); the 'path' is the working out of this tension, not by choosing one or the other, but by reconciling them in a higher-order organization whose full quality as a value (goal) emerges out of the tension being worked out. There is, at every stage and at every moment, an interdependence of process and structure.

The fact that these 'conductors' are more of the nature of transactional flow-patterns that can be understood as 'cognitions, appreciations, discernments' (*shes-rab*) on the input side, and as 'experiments, adaptations, actions' (*thabs*) on the output side, held together by the common (open-ended) flow-pattern in which the differentiation into the two aspects (input-output) of the process no longer holds—although at any moment it may so emerge—is borne out by the definition of the 'conductors'. Speaking of definition, it must be borne in mind that 'conductors' are illustrative of the processes taking place, not demonstrative of static entities. Furthermore, as transactional flow-patterns they have no particular point where they begin or end, and it is merely a more or less arbitrary decision to start with the 'conductor' termed *ro-ma* and then to continue with the *rkyang-ma* and *kun-'dar-ma*. We have to start somewhere, and since the discussion of these 'conductors' is tied in with the morphogenesis of the individual, it is obvious that there has taken place an 'input' (the genetic code) before the 'output' (the explication of the genetic code) began, and yet this same output is being, and has been, checked and reaffirmed by the 'input'. To the extent that the output matches the information input, it is felt and experienced as 'positive' while, when it does not, it is 'negative'. This accounts for the apparently contradictory definitions of *ro-ma*:

> It is similar to salt because it seasons everything, and so it is called *ro* ('flavor'), because on the basis of the optimally felt value (*bde-ba*) of the bioenergetic flow-input (*thig-le*) it sets up an uncommon (feeling) experience; and it is called *ma* ('bottom'), because it starts from 'desire-attachment', (which is the reason that) those who have desire-attachment can, on the basis of this desire-attachment, grow up to Buddhahood. On the other hand, *ro* ('corpse') means little activity, and since the (feeling) experience, on the basis of the bioenergetic flow-input's having gone wrong, is difficult to express in words, it is called *ma* ('negative'). It is through this 'conductor' that the bioenergetic input as reproductivity moves, and hence this 'conductor' is of the nature of 'action' (*thabs*).[25]

The intimate connection between 'action' and, as we may say, the 'information input', expressed in the above illustrative definition, highlights another significant aspect of this transactional process. 'Action' is amplifying and exploratory and can assume many forms of 'output', which matches the information input or not. In any case, it depends on a steady flow of 'input' that must not diminish into 'dead ends' or be 'slanted'. Consequently the *rkyang-ma* is described as follows:

Since there are neither bends nor branches in it, it is *rkyang*, 'simple', 'solitary'. Being actually the source of both the bioenergetic input as it is experienced as input, and the bioenergetic input as it is accepted and felt as reproductivity, it brings to maturity and separates from one another the elemental forces as forces and as products. Since it is simple, it does not undergo changes. Since it is the foundation of everything, it is *ma*, 'mother'. It is through this facet that a person can grow up to Buddhahood effortlessly.[26]

Because of its definition as 'simple' and 'solitary' we may be misled into the assumption that there is little creativity in this flow-process. Actually, correlated to the control centers set up in the course of the process referred to as *ro-ma*, there are similar control centers that have to do with the deepening or intensification of the experience referred to by the 'lamps' that spread their light through the process termed *rkyang-ma*.[27]

Both the processes and structures of *ro-ma* and *rkyang-ma* (when seen as 'conductors') have their unity in the *kun-'dar-ma* which is described in the following manner:

kun-'dar-ma means 'to combine everything'. While *kun* ('everything') is so called because, on the basis of this (conductor as process), everything—the bioenergetic input as well as the optimally felt value of the conductors and the optimally felt value of 'motility'—comes into operation, it is because of its all-encompassing features in the most general way that it is called *'dar-ma* ('vibrating').[28]

This all-encompassing feature is, like everything else, thoroughly dynamic as is evident from the additional information about the 'conductor':

(In the) *kun-'dar-ma* the nature of all 'conductors' is summed up. It is 'vibrating' (*'dar-ba*) with the oscillating flux of motility, and it is 'motherly' (*ma*), because (thereby) it has become the foundation of both Saṃsāra and Nirvāṇa.[29]

Because of this dynamic view that pervades the whole conception of man's nature, his 'samsaric' and 'nirvanic' states are something like an alternating current phenomenon, so that the *kun-'dar-ma* may be seen as the 'current' with the *ro-ma* and *rkyang-ma* as the respective phases. The *ro-ma* is the 'bioenergetic input' at work as it is observed physiologically, and which, being merely a phase of the current, retains the nature of the 'current' which, by contrast, is psychic. The *rkyang-ma* is creative in being a high-frequency phenomenon, and also 'intelligent' as it sets up the organism's complex order of 'conductors'. This seems to be what Klong-chen rab-'byams-pa has in mind when he elaborates:

> The wide-ranging openness that comes from the 'central conductor' without there being blood or lymph is 'motility in action' (*rlung-gi las*). Since through the right conductor lymph and blood and *byang-sems* move, this is 'bioenergy in action' (*thig-le'i las*), and since through the left conductor the radiation energy of the elemental forces as well as *ye-shes* proceed, this is the 'conductors in action' (*rtsa rang-gi las*).[30]

The significance of this passage lies in the fact that the triad of 'conductors', 'motility', and 'bioenergetic input' is presented here in still another perspective that makes any reductionist concretization impossible. No less significant is the contrast between *byang-sems* and *ye-shes*. The latter term can easily be rendered as the 'wisdom of the body' which, as the neuroanatomical 'order' of the organism, leads us to an understanding of what lies beyond that which we know how to analyze. The former is the trend towards recapturing the optimal value of being which, intellectually, we see and feel as the thrust for limpid clearness and consummate perspicacity, and which is, physiologically, the organism's reproductive capacity triggering the morphogenesis of a 'new' organism. Both the density or condensation process and the high frequency or radiation process are a manifestation of a pervasive 'current'.

However baffling, at first glance, this highly technical terminology may appear, because it combines what we have split into opposites, it is obvious that, in all these instances, interacting *dynamic* processes are at work, and that the boundary between 'action' and 'cognition', to mention only two of the most salient processes, is indeed fuzzy. Still something clear-cut and accurate can be said in the realm of experience which is brought to life again by what is, quite inadequately, called 'meditation'.

We can speak of 'action' (*thabs*), as it proceeds 'objectively' and is described 'factually' as 'pleasure' (*bde-ba*), since it represents an optimally felt value in experience. It will be noticed that already here the gap between 'fact' (as isolated object) and 'value' (as subject's response) is bridged. This bridging is itself a process and is related to the process indicated by the *ro-ma*.

We can speak further of a second and even larger process that occurs 'subjectively' through our cognitions and appreciations, which are not something static or concrete. There is, however, no knowing without acting as there is no acting without knowing. Knowing (appreciating, discriminating) is always unique, never some 'thing' or other; it is 'open' (*stong-pa*) and therefore it is not a 'subject' in the ordinary sense of the word. Through the uniqueness of cognition as a process the notion of 'subject' (I, self) is resolved. This is the work of the *rkyang-ma*.

Lastly, we can speak of a still larger process which may be called 'totality process', of which and in which our 'cognitive processes', as well as our 'actional processes', are occurrences which have the tendency to break up into separate areas. The totality process, *kun-'dar-ma*, is the immediacy out of which both the 'subjective' and the 'objective' are drawn and to which they point:

> The *ro-ma* is pleasure, and having a specific activity it sets the 'objective' free in pure meaningfulness; the *rkyang-ma* is openness, and through pure appreciation sets the 'subjective'

free in pure meaningfulness; and the *kun-'dar-ma* is the unity of pleasure and openness, and through this union reveals the pristine cognitiveness, that is free from the subjective and objective, to have no gaps.[31]

'Action' and 'cognition' are two processes superseded, as it were, and held together by a 'totality process' which holds the balance between the two other processes or, to state it more precisely, balances them out by being in the middle.

To speak of the *kun-'dar-ma* as balancing out the two processes designated as 'action' and 'appreciation' indirectly emphasizes the role this 'conductor' plays in the development of the bilateral symmetry, which points to an orientation towards an environment which is both external and internal and, hence, shaped in interaction. Nonetheless, in this orientation towards an environment as 'life-world', the cognitive phase of 'appreciation', which by its very nature is discerning and discriminative, takes precedence over 'action' which is experimental. There must be 'information' before something can be 'worked out'. But even this latter phase is, in a certain sense, information too, insofar as it tells a person how it is going with him, whether the goal-directed and, incidentally, goal-inspired action is moving in the direction of the goal or not. But while the information input moves in a steady flow, the working out of this input has its ups and downs, and while this working out of the information flow that is steadily pouring in may be viewed as the 'objective' component, real enough in an operational sense (*kun-rdzob*), but secondary to the 'subjective' component, it is this latter component that is 'primary' (*don-dam*), not as a static 'ego' or 'self' or 'I', but as a process of experiencing (perceiving, knowing, appreciating) without whose accuracy our 'objective' world would not even be operationally reliable. However, both the 'objective' and the 'subjective' operate in a larger field, the totality of our individuality, constantly interacting and continuously being 'fed' with meanings that remain strictly within and come out of this totality, in the sense that this totality is with us all the time and yet nowhere, is without time and yet is every instant of time. As the problem under consideration is *living* man, not a lifeless abstraction, it is not by accident that this 'feeding' is said to be bioenergetic and, as sheer lucency, a high-frequency vibration whose inner content is 'meaning' and which is 'decoded' by pristine cognitions which are an equally bioenergetic process, and 'worked out' by a bioenergetic feedback. This will help us in understanding Klong-chen rab-'byams-pa's concise statement:

> In the *ro-ma* there is what is real in a general and operational sense (*kun-rdzob*), the bioenergetic process triggering (related processes, *rgyu'i thig-le*) whose nature is 'action' (*thabs*) and whose felt value (*bde-ba*) is unsteady. In the *rkyang-ma* there is what is primary (*don-dam*), the bioenergetic process of pristine cognitiveness (*ye-shes-kyi thig-le*) whose nature is 'appreciative' (*shes-rab*) and whose felt value remains steady. In the *kun-'dar-ma* there is what it is actually about (*rang-bzhin*), the bioenergetic process of meaningfulness (*chos-nyid-kyi thig-le*) whose nature is spontaneously present sheer lucency, the non-duality of the totality-field (*dbyings*) and its pristine cognitiveness (*ye-shes*).[32]

Diagrammatically, this is shown in Figure 2.

The complexity of all these 'conductors' as specific pathways along which the bioenergetic input is carried, together with the control centers at the various stages of the process, is also known as the 'energy body' (*rdo-rje'i lus*).[33] On the one hand, it influences the working of an individual's mind and physical body which represent distinct energy patterns, and, on the other, it links each individual with the whole of Being. This is indicated by reference to another 'conductor'-pattern[34] which is no less complex than the triadic one discussed here, because of the significance that attention to this 'energy body' has for the optimal life performance of and by an individual.

FIGURE 2

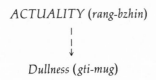

ACTUALITY (*rang-bzhin*)

↓

Dullness (*gti-mug*)

'CENTRAL' FLOW-PATTERN

(*kun-'dar-ma*)

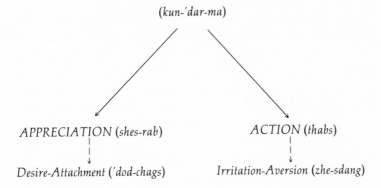

APPRECIATION (*shes-rab*)   *ACTION* (*thabs*)

↓   ↓

Desire-Attachment (*'dod-chags*)   *Irritation-Aversion* (*zhe-sdang*)

'LEFT' FLOW-PATTERN ⟷ 'RIGHT' FLOW-PATTERN

(*rkyang-ma*)   (*ro-ma*)

(1) The 'primary' process (*don-dam*) is *ACTUALITY*, *APPRECIA-TION*, and *ACTION*.

(2) The 'operationally valid' process (*kun-rdzob*) is *Dullness*, *Desire-Attachment*, and *Irritation-Aversion*.

(3) '– – →' indicates the change which takes place in the transition from 'primary' to 'operationally-valid' processes.

(4) '——→', '←——→' indicate the dynamic 'flow' between the 'CEN-TRAL', 'LEFT', and 'RIGHT' FLOW-PATTERNS or 'conductors' (*rtsa*).

The primary process is immediately present in experience and is the 'starting point' of all interpretations belonging to the operationally valid process. Both processes are active 'within' and 'through' the conductors or flow-patterns.

Related to this problem of the 'energy body' being an intermediary is the question about its origin. Surprisingly the answer is already contained in the definition of the 'energy body' as being thoroughly dynamic with nothing static whatsoever about it, and in the distinction between that which is real enough in an operational sense (*kun-rdzob*), as this is what is commonly observable and 'objective' and in the foreground, and that which is primary (*don-dam*) but less easily accessible and hence 'subjective' and in the background—as far as the concrete living individual is concerned, who, after all, through his 'subjective' component remains linked with the 'totality field' (*rang-bzhin*) that is his 'existence'. But this totality field is itself linked to an even larger field so that the one commonly dealt with in its triadic pattern of the 'conductors' is operationally real, while the larger field having high-frequency radiation by virtue of its 'sheer lucency' (*'od-gsal*), remains and acts as being primary.

The consequence of this idea is that the 'energy body' does not start abruptly at the moment of some initial time t_0, but that this moment marks the separation of the total interaction. This separation involves a drop in the frequency of radiation and leads to one-half of the totality having less energy which, figuratively speaking, is said to belong to 'our side'. In rDzogs-chen thinking this drop is known as *ma-rig-pa*, 'loss in *rig-pa*', 'loss in pure awareness'. The term 'pure awareness' (*rig-pa*) indicates the 'intelligent' nature of the universe of which man is, so to say, a low-frequency manifestation. In other words, 'cognitiveness' in all its primacy (*ye-shes*) has become 'emotiveness' (*nyon-mongs*) with 'dullness' (*gti-mug*) predominating.

The most important and stimulating aspect of these ideas is that what happens on 'our' side has a relationship to what happens on the 'other' side. That which happens on the other side, in approaching the moment t_0 seems to be able to maintain its coherence as it passes through t_0. Yet as it passes into 'our' side it becomes a kind of 'blurred primacy'—the 'subjective' component in the 'energy body' reaching into our concrete world of subject-object distinctions. The state of affairs on 'our side' is thus subject to control by, and owes much of what goes on in ourselves to what happens on the 'other side'. Once it is on 'our side', the operating forces bring about a distortion of what has come. The interesting point to note here is that much of our present situation is due to the situation on the far side of that boundary which has hitherto been thought to represent the origin of our being. Thus Klong-chen rab-'byams-pa declares,

> Although the 'energy body' is shown as a triad of conductors, motility, and bioenergetic input, actually it is not found to be different from the facticity of the unitary pristine cognitiveness. As is stated in the *Rig-pa rang-shar chen-po'i rgyud*:
>
>> Even the conductors, motility, and bioenergetic input
>> Are not such as to have passed beyond the reach and
>>   range of pristine cognitiveness.
>
> Therefore, even at the time of impurity, they have not passed beyond the triad of facticity, actuality, and responsiveness, as is stated in the *Seng-ge rtsal-rdzogs chen-po'i rgyud*:
>
>> In all the sentient beings of all the three spheres,
>> There resides the triple hierarchy of the essential
>>   cognitiveness.[35]

He gives a more elaborate account of the dynamic process in its ramifications, even as it takes place on 'our side', in the following words:

> In this area which is real enough in an operational sense (*kun-rdzob*), the three conductors derive from a loss in 'pure awareness' and form the basis for 'desire-attachment' on the left side, for 'irritation-aversion' on the right side, and for 'dullness' in the center; the *shel-sbug-can*[36] does not form a basis for anything that is 'impure'. In the time that is primary (to this development) they are, generally speaking, estab-

lished by the dynamics of pristine cognitiveness, in particular, as 'action' (*thabs*) on the right side, 'appreciation' (*shes-rab*)
on the left side, and as their unity in the center.[37]

Taking these two passages together we may illuminate
them by drawing from recent findings in astronomy. Let us
assume that the moment t_0 represents the moment that separates positive interactions from negative ones, and let us
call the negative ones 'the other side' since the interactions
taking place there are not directly observable. Let us further
assume that what happens on the 'other side' is similar to
what happens on 'our side'. When what happens on the
'other side'—the interaction between facticity, actuality, and
responsiveness—draws nearer the moment t_0 and passes
through it, it retains its identity of the 'other side' but its
radiation is 'blurred' into the interaction of 'action', 'appreciation', and their 'unity'. It is this blurred interaction which
is detectable and which, as such, is similar to what as-
tronomers call 'microwave background radiation'. When
this movement reaches the moment t_1, (in addition to becoming blurred) it is deflected by what I shall call the 'psychological red-shift', which accounts for the fact that 'pristine cognitiveness', in its passage through t_0 and proceeding
to t_1, becomes 'emotiveness'. That is to say, just as with each
passing moment the successive photons emitted from re-
ceding galaxies have farther to travel to reach the earth so
that their rate of arrival is slower than it would have been if
the galaxy had been stationary, and in the same way as the
Doppler effect accounts for the shift of photons to lower
frequencies so that they have less energy, so also the 'light
values of the various kinds of pristine cognitiveness' deriving
from 'sheer lucency' in moving away from t_0 to $t_1, t_2, \ldots t_n$
take longer to reach us (who are likewise not stationary) so
that their brightness is dimmed and the shift to lower frequencies gives the 'emotions' their specific colors.

The following diagram attempts to illustrate this interaction in highly schematized form:

FIGURE 3

direction of 'temporal' flow

| B | desire-attachment ('dod-chags) ↔ | dullness-lusterlessness (gti-mug) ↔ | irritation-aversion (zhe-sdang) | 'this' side | operationally valid process (Kun-rdzob) |

t_1 —————|—————|————— t_1

A(a) appreciation (shes-rab) ⟷ action (thabs)
actuality (rang-bzhin)

t_0 ——————————————— t_0

A actuality (rang-bzhin)
facticity (ngo-bo) ← – – – – → responsiveness (thugs-rje) 'other' side primary process (don-dam)

(1) During 'A', which characterizes the dynamics of the 'other side' up to the initial moment t_0, 'facticity' (ngo-bo), an utter openness, is present in and as 'actuality' (rang-bzhin), a pure radiance, which solicits and receives 'responsiveness' (thugs-rje) or resonance, a pristine cognitiveness.
'← – – – →' indicates the interconnectedness of these dynamics which cannot be further specified.

(2) 'A(a)' represents what takes place between t_0 and t_1. At t_0 it seems that the bare presence of the dynamic patternings in 'A' has developed to such a degree that 'actuality' crosses over, thereby initiating a development which we can call 'this side'. After t_0 'actuality' is present as a sustaining and holding together of the dialectical movement between 'appreciation' (shes-rab) as information input, and 'action' (thabs) as the developmental and morphogenetic unfolding of this input.

(3) 'B' represents what takes place after moment t_1 and may be characterized as a kind of 'red shift' in which 'actuality' operates as 'dullness-lusterlessness' (gti-mug), 'appreciation' operates as 'desire-attachment' ('dod-chags), and 'action' operates as 'irritation-aversion' (zhe-sdang). In psychological terms the situation after t_1 is one in which we are alienated from ourselves.

'⟷' indicates that a triadic interrelatedness operates in all situations after t_0 (that is, in both A(a), and B).

A and A(a) are 'primary' processes (don-dam); B is the 'operationally valid' process (kun-rdzob).

When Klong-chen rab-'byams-pa goes on to say that

> At the period of the path (these three conductors) form the basis for pleasure (*bde-ba*) on the left side, for radiance (*gsal-ba*) on the right side, and for non-dividedness (*mi-rtog-pa*) in the center,[38]

he points to the phenomenon which indicates in which direction the process is going, and which helps a person to see that he is moving in the right direction. It is these phenomena, therefore, that are specifically discussed in this part of the Trilogy. 'Giving in' to the emotions is a waste and, as we would say, 'entropic' in character; 'tuning in' to the bioenergetic process is to activate man's potential, or, as Klong-chen rab-'byams-pa says,

> At the goal (these conductors) form the basis for the founding stratum of meaning (*chos-sku*) in the center, for the founding strata of a world-horizon (*longs-sku*) and of bearers of apprehendable meaning (*sprul-sku*) on the right side, and the basis for absolute pleasure, sheer lucency, as infinite as the sky, on the left side.[39]

The interrelation of these phenomena may be seen diagrammatically in Figure 4.

It seems as if the prevailing and, on the whole, symmetrical arrangement and ordering of the processes taking place in and characterizing the growth of an individual, has been given up when the level of the 'goal' is reached. Here, from among the three founding strata—that of meaning (*chos-sku*), of engagement in a world-horizon saturated with meaning (*longs-sku*), and of embodiments of meaning (*sprul-sku*)—the founding stratum of meaning, as should be expected, is in the center. On the level of the path, this represented the non-dividedness of radiance and pleasure as indicators that the process or 'path' went as it was meant to proceed, and which, in the 'primary' or 'subjective' level (as contrasted with the operationally real and 'objective' level with the emotional vagaries that characterize the body-speech-mind

FIGURE 4

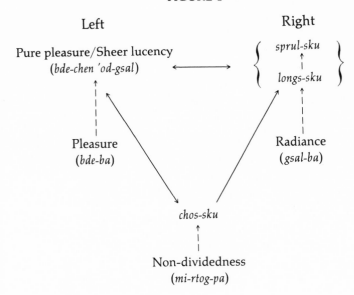

'– – →' indicates 'leads to'

'←——→' indicates 'interacts with'

'———→' indicates 'develops as'

The 'path' encompasses: *bde-ba, gsal-ba,* and *mi-rtog-pa.*

The 'goal' encompasses: *bde-chen 'od-gsal, chos-sku* (also present on and as the 'path'), *longs-sku,* and *sprul-sku.*

configuration of the person), represented the unity of 'action' and 'appreciation' (remaining dialectically related while the emotions are in open conflict).

The two other founding strata are said to be on the right side. Both of them are such that the one follows out of the other, and both of them are 'primary' in the sense that as existential experiences they lend themselves to 'secondary' concretizations and descriptions as lifeless abstractions which are the domain of the 'objective' contents of mind. As to their 'primacy', they are truly on the side of 'action' inasmuch as they themselves are the enactment of the 'central meaning'. But on the left side there is no founding stratum, rather there is 'absolute pleasure, sheer lucency' which operates through, while remaining beyond, 'appreciation' which is already the creation of the creativity (*rtsal*) that is pristine cognitiveness (*ye-shes*). This, in turn, is sheer lucency and pure pleasure which we may experience as that which makes us become a 'founding stratum' (*sku*). A 'founding stratum' is a knowingly-felt 'presence', and as such belongs to the thematic-reflective aspect of experience, rather than to that which makes this aspect possible. As Klong-chen rab-'byams-pa remarks:

> While the ordinary spiritual pursuit claims the three founding strata to be the goal, the rDzogs-chen teaching claims them to be the 'presence of the path' (*lam-gyi snang-ba*). Even the founding stratum of meaning (*chos-sku*) is but a 'presence of the path'. As long as there is 'meaning' (*chos*), there is the intellect (*blo*) and this involves the path. As long as there is a 'founding stratum' (*sku*), there is the living body (*lus*) (as founding stratum for the intellect), and this, too, is a presence of the path. It is not the ultimate.[40]

Thus, what in the previously quoted passage seemed to be an unequal distribution of the three founding strata in the prevalent triadic pattern (of pleasure, non-dividedness, and radiance) has turned out to be an accurate observation. A goal that is a dead end because it is a referent of the intellect is not a goal worth the name for 'cognitive systems' as represented by a living person.

The 'path' as a continuing process involving the whole person, makes itself known and felt and apprehendable in the phenomena of pleasure, radiance, and non-dividedness which as phenomena and indices attract the person's attention and, for this reason, lend themselves to become misidentified as 'what meditation is all about'. Non-dividedness (*mi-rtog-pa*) is not a mere absence of divisive concepts and of thought in general, but, figuratively speaking, is the situation of having risen above the dichotomies set up and multiplied by divisive concepts, and hence makes us know more. It is integrative of the splits within the individual. Since an individual is not in a vacuum, non-dividedness is also integrative of the splits between one individual and another, and between individuals and their environment. In being integrative it is central and centering, and therefore it is related to the central 'conductor' in the 'energy body'. Because of the attention it attracts it may easily be misidentified through interference by the intellect and, speaking in a very broad way, be turned into 'dullness' which, as an induced state of proverbial blankness of the mind, leaves the person who pursues such a course worse off than he was before.

Pleasure (*bde-ba*) is not merely a bodily sensation, but is more an indication of a person's mood. It would be rather difficult to be pleasurably excited and to enjoy some situation while one is divided against oneself. Pleasure therefore is felt and grows in intensity as the dissociative tendencies are overcome. Because of its informative character, telling us how things are going with us, it is on the left in the 'energy body', as this side is related to 'appreciation'. Pleasure is strongly 'felt' in the body as the common ground upon which sex and love meet. However, to separate sex and love and then to go on to define the one as 'biological' and 'operational', and the other as 'psychological' and 'appreciative', shows a dissociative tendency which leads to a misidentification of pleasure as sex-and-sex-only because of the undeniable presence of the body. A preoccupation with the body, usually coupled with fear and anxiety about it, reveals a peculiar naiveté, and, in Klong-chen rab-'byams-pa's words, is characteristic of a person of low intelligence. On the other hand, to reject the 'body' and to indulge in 'sentiments of love' is no less dissociative, although it admits of something other than just the physical body. Still, these sentiments borrow their imagery from the physical. Like non-dividedness, pleasure is irreducible; it informs and shapes the personality and for this reason cannot be commanded.

Correlated with pleasure is radiance (*gsal-ba*), which is an aspect of motility and excitation. While pleasure is appreciative, radiance is operational in the sense that it is 'working out' the information that is steadily pouring in. Therefore radiance is associated with the right in the 'energy body', as it is this side that acts and works out. This active and operational quality is noticeable in any living individual. A person is 'glowing' when he is at his best. But to be at one's best means not to be dissociated and divided, and by implication, not to be depressed or unhappy. The moment dissociative tendencies reassert themselves, as when 'appreciation' is turned into a cold judgment of 'fact' by the intellect, not only is pleasure reduced, but radiance is quickly lost. The eyes no longer 'sparkle', the complexion of the skin is pasty, and there is a general lack of aliveness. Radiance is a 'steady' quality and must not be confused or misidentified with a sudden glow that may occur in the rush of an emotion. Such misidentification would merely intensify an already dissociated state.

Precisely because it is through pleasure, radiance, and non-dividedness that we can learn about ourselves, they can never be considered as and must never be made an end in themselves. To do so would effectively block the very possibility of ever learning more about ourselves. It is for this reason that their positive (negentropic) as well as negative (entropic) features, which as an in-built tension energize the individual to pursue his path through life, are discussed at great length with reference to the individual's 'intelligence', which is not something uniform but varies from individual to individual. Pleasure, radiance, and non-dividedness, each in its own way, and even more so jointly, aid in the development of a particular capacity for understanding ourselves and of a particular attitude that makes such understanding more feasible. They are thus that aspect of life which enables us to make the 'big jump' to where we become the stream of life itself. To be this stream itself is, in rDzogs-chen thought and practice, *bsam-gtan* which we have seen indicates only mediately what is meant by the English word 'meditation'. Everything else is the exercise of 'creative imagination', 'contemplative attention' (*sgom-pa*), which could be called 'meditation' in a very loose way.

'Creative imagination' is a way of thinking of and attending to something present by thinking of it, or even perceiving it, in terms of something absent. The thoughts and feelings that are so aroused become part of the experience itself and transform it without diverting it from what has been initially present. Being of the nature of thinking it is related to both concentration and conception. 'Concentration' involves something upon which the mind is focussed or centered to the exclusion of everything else. It has, so to speak, something concrete to deal with (*rten-can*). 'Imagination' does not have something concrete (*rten-med*), yet it is the capacity by which we become aware of something present (*snang-bcas*), of something which, lacking 'concreteness', belongs to the inner life. 'Conception' deals with what may never show up (*snang-med*). I can imagine an 'energy body' as I can concentrate on a painting, but I can neither imagine nor concentrate on emptiness although I can conceive of it. Thus the common feature of concentration, imagination, and conception is that they are primarily referential, but insofar as they are processes they may approach the non-referential phase, in which dividedness into subject-object seems to have been overcome. Actually, the division has merely been suspended temporarily, and the 'big jump' from the subjective realm to the totality realm has not yet been made.

'Creative imagination' (*sgom-pa*) may give us a glimpse of what it might mean to be the stream of life maintaining its continuous forward thrust, but it is not this stream. And yet it is this stream that matters. Making this 'big jump' by which we become the stream itself, no longer remaining its onlookers, is *bsam-gtan*, 'becoming the stream in being the

stream'. Thus the distinction between *sgòm-pa* (creative imagination, contemplative attention, 'meditation', abstract con-
ceiving) and *bsam-gtan* (the experience of totality in and
through the totality of Being) is of paramount importance. As
Klong-chen rab-'byams-pa explains:[41]

> Many gradations in the objective reference as a means to
> guide the average person within the ordinary spiritual pur-
> suits, and here in the (rDzogs-chen way) the less fortunate
> ones, have been discussed. But they all can be subsumed
> under pursuing an objective reference which either has
> something concrete about it (*rten-can*) or not (*rten-med*). That
> which has something concrete about it (*rten-can*) involves a
> steady concentration of the mind on anything that is an object
> of the external world such as a colored patch, a sound, a fra-
> grance, a tactile pressure and so on; it also involves concen-
> trating the mind on the figure of a god, (his or her) symbols, a
> small piece of wood or a pebble. That which has nothing
> concrete about itself (*rten-med*) is an object of subjective
> (imaginative) thinking. Insofar as it deals with what is 'felt' as
> a presence (*snang-bcas*), it involves the claim of not giving in to
> conceptualization when the mind has been concentrated on
> each or any objective reference referred to as 'conductor',
> 'motility', or 'bioenergetic input', and it also involves such
> objective references as syllabic sound symbols, globules of
> light, control centers within the conductors, the fire of inner
> heat, and so on. It is concentrating the mind on the gradation
> of the imaginative thinking process. If it is a matter of nothing
> showing up (*snang-med*), it involves sitting cross-legged and
> projecting the mind into a state where no concepts enter and
> holding it there absolutely motionless. This state of utter
> blankness is an objective reference that is not conceptually
> objectifiable. In general terms, the statement that an objective
> reference is either conceptually objectifiable or not belongs to
> this feature. In brief, any claim that something is referential is
> a product of imagination. It is a steadying of the mind, an
> expectation of a result through its steadiness, and its function
> is the suspension of the subject-object dichotomy. In the *sGra
> thal-'gyur chen-po'i rgyud*[42] it has been stated:

Creative imagination means to have the mind in a
   steady state
And to cut off any outward or inward movement.
It is the suspension of the subject-object dichotomy.
And,
   Furthermore, (attending to) the conductors, motility,
      bioenergetic input,
   Vital spots in the body, and emptiness
   Are claimed to be creative imagination.[43]

Since all this, precisely because of its claim to suspend the
subject-object dichotomy, lets the objective reference become an object and the intellect a subject, it is not the being
tuned-in into the profoundness of one's being; rather, it is
merely a means to bring a person to his profound nature.

The specificity of *bsam-gtan* in rDzogs-chen thought and
practice is that in the same way as there is heat in its own right
as long as there is fire, or moisture throughout in water, so
also there is *bsam-gtan* throughout with respect to 'pure
awareness' (*rig-pa*). As long as 'pure awareness' is experien-
tially encountered, one stays in what is *bsam-gtan* steeped
throughout in itself. Hence, the experience of pleasure, radiance, and non-dividedness comes by itself and naturally
rather than by being contrived. Similarly the experience of
the intermediate and reorganizatory state comes as such a
state settled throughout in itself as 'pure awareness'. As long
as one deals with 'mind' (*sems*), the experience that imagines
the mind to be in a steady state is set up with effort and is
going to break down, and this is as it is (wherever the mind is
involved). As long as one deals with pristine cognitiveness
(which is) 'pure awareness' (in operation), one stays in the
stream that is *bsam-gtan*, steeped throughout in itself, and
hence the capabilities that have come into operation naturally
remain such that throughout time they are inseparable.

And so it is in *bsam-gtan*, the experience of totality in and
through the totality of Being, that we may find comfort and
ease, while it is the preoccupation with *sems*, the mind as the
noetic-noematic complex with its built-in limitations and
disruptive tendencies, that has us worried.

CHAPTER ONE

The Environment

To an alarming degree modern man has lost his sense of place, this delicate awareness of a mute and deep affinity with the environment. In the Western world this loss is due to a one-sided, ideologically misdirected approach to the problem of man and the universe, and in the East this calamitous approach is readily followed and hailed as progress. This disastrous disorientation has started from the assumption of a permanent separation between subject and object, the observer and the observed. Following its own logic, it has taken an impersonal and allegedly value-free stance which nevertheless is tainted by modern (Western) man's inheritance of the medieval delight in the corruption of the flesh. This latter, being of the same stuff as 'nature' (and in contrast with 'spirit', which is 'abstract' and pure), is seen as dirty, alien, hostile, and evil, and hence in need of being conquered, subjugated, and disinfected. As a consequence, nature or man's environment lies outside the range of ethical responsibility for human action upon it.

Although modern man may deceive himself into believing that he has outgrown this medieval superstition and that all he does now is merely to assess the world 'objectively' and impersonally, his supposedly 'rational' approach remains essentially wishful and artificial. It is 'wishful' in the sense that the underlying assumption, that all that has been excluded from the live world is of no relevance for the abstract model of the world measured in quantitative terms, will not be noticed and exposed for what it is—a mere assumption. It is 'artificial' in the sense that the formalization of arbitrarily selected aspects of reality into supposedly 'objective' truth remains a 'subjective' construction if not a painful distortion. However, regardless of whether or not we extol 'objectivity' and denounce 'subjectivity'—and we should not pretend that we do this on purely 'rational' grounds—we merely exhibit a state of 'having-gone-astray' ('*khrul-pa*').

This fact of 'having-gone-astray', as well as our propensity for continually 'going astray' into the debris of dead and deadening postulates, are not inescapable patterns of human existence (envisaged either as a closed equilibrium system with monotonously increasing entropy in the terms of physics, or as a state of fallenness from which man is unable to rise by himself, in the terms of traditional Western religion). The propensity for going astray, rather, implies the possibility of 'finding one's way back to', and again being 'in tune with', the very source of our being, which can never be a static absolute.

Such a possibility, therefore, does not maintain a separation between man and the universe, nor does it reinforce our dividedness against ourselves, which is the outcome of our 'having-gone-astray'. Instead, it helps to heal self-inflicted wounds by deeply involving us in the process of rediscovering the identity of the forces operating in the observer and the observed world. In this process we encounter and respond to a wealth of qualities which, in turn, are the outcome of the interaction between the 'material' without—the forces that, as forces, solicit a response—and the 'psychic' within—the forces that, as forces in responding to these solicitations, bestow fresh meaning upon the interaction taking place. This interaction brings into the foreground feelings through which we communicate with life: in the interpersonal domain through love and compassion (and also hatred), and in our natural environment by resonance (and also dissonance), by being 'in tune' (and 'out of tune') with biorhythms as exemplified by the seasons.

Such communication takes on the character of a personal relationship between man and his environment. It becomes 'anthropomorphic' in the sense that nature not only speaks to man, be it in a friendly or hostile, gentle or stern, reassuring or threatening way, but is also spoken to and 'acted upon' in the same manner. Thus feelings of calmness, expansion, powerfulness, severity and oppressiveness, which some places may inspire, are the direct experience of the working of the self-realizing and self-organizing creative unity of man and world, the 'Buddha overall intentionality' within and through each of us, a totality that is inclusive in not having a subject-world dichotomy and is a timeless now-and-here.

This experience comes to us in images of 'gods' or 'goddesses', of malignant demons or enchanting nymphs, and through the appreciation of these images we gain knowledge about the features of, for example, a place or an object. Images are kinds of thought, exhibiting the same intentionality as thought and being known as immediately as thoughts. In effect, then, this knowledge about certain features has two dimensions: one of thought, and one of experience. As thought it may be expressed in a propositional construction; as experience it may be paraphrased as being the sensory 'embodiment' of what otherwise is merely a 'thought'. We may 'think of' a place as having a languorous atmosphere and express it in the appropriate proposition, but we may also 'experience' this languorousness as an enchantress—alluring, charming and fascinating—the sensuous and sensual 'embodiment' of our thoughts.

It is through experience, which may be triggered by any encounter with reality, or in the narrower sense, by the place in which man lives as part of reality and with which he interacts, that he feels the dynamic forces of the universe acting through him. In exercising these forces creatively he defines himself as well as his place in and relationship to the world. This creative exercise, which does not occur in a vacuum nor even at random, is technically known as the 'Developing Stage' and the 'Fulfillment Stage', in the exercise of which both deterministic and finalistic principles are at work.

In order to define oneself and one's place in the world, to reach one's goal (regardless of whether we conceive of it in static or dynamic terms), deterministic (intentional) processes have to be set up, such as those covered by the term 'Developing Stage'. Nevertheless these practices are guided from the direction of the goal, not in the sense of involving a final cause, but of being concerned with tendencies towards a terminus whose constancy or steady state is one of a continuous flow of component material, such as is referred to by the term 'Fulfillment Stage'. The former, by virtue of being a creative process, involves anticipatory action which aims towards ever renewed spiritual life by devising feasible paradigms. This becomes evident from what Klong-chen rab-'byams-pa has to say about the Developing Stage:[1]

> Thus the external world is to be a (Buddha) realm and the sentient beings are to be deities;
> One's own body is to be a beautiful palace, one's speech a first utterance,[2]
> And one's mind the radiance of divinity—thereby preoccupation with the ordinary ceases.
> Still, the stains of the obscurations that accompany the continuum (of experience and Being) have not been burnt away.

The Developing Stage is a step in the direction of greater psychic receptivity manifest as qualitative patterns. It is an 'opening up' in establishing relationships with both people and the non-personal world. But while the Developing Stage merely indicates man's relating to a world or reality in whose shaping he is actively participating, it is the appreciativeness of the Fulfillment Stage which constitutes the determinative principle and which gives increased meaning to our actions and our world without rigidifying either. It is only a manner of speaking when we say that the Fulfillment Stage 'follows' the Developing Stage:

> Thereafter comes the cultivation of the Fulfillment Stage,
> Mind-as-such as unobjectifiable meaningfulness and
>   Mind-as-such as sheer lucency.
> This is the intention of the Tantras dealing with
>   ultimate certainty.[3]

As Klong-chen rab-'byams-pa explains, in the Developing Stage we are still 'on the surface' and the 'surface' still obscures the 'depth' of our Being; in the Fulfillment Stage we are not only 'in the midst of reality', we have penetrated to the 'depth', to 'reality' itself:[4]

> Having had on the previous stage our mind blaze forth as a god, here Mind-as-such is cultivated as Fulfillment Stage, which is to make the founding stratum of apprehendable meaning and the founding stratum of meaningfulness,[5] aesthetic presence and the open dimension of Being, the way. Ignorant persons, claiming the rambling of the mind and the concrete forms of content it assumes to be the Fulfillment Stage, are mistaken because they make the aesthetic presence and the concrete forms of content it takes, their operational field. Fulfillment means to make the open dimension of Being and its unconcretizable meaningfulness the operational field.

While there is interplay of action and appreciation, both being experiences of a self-regulating and self-transcending process, there is also, seen from another perspective, an interplay of man and his environment—whether this be of the 'natural' kind or of his own making—which is ultimately designed to facilitate his 'tuning in' to that wider reality which he intuitively knows and feels to be his real home.

Praise to Śrī Samantabhadra[6]

Homage from within the ground, complete,
    neither stepping out of itself into a different
    realm nor changing into something other
    than itself,
To this very core of limpid clearness and consummate
    perspicacity, sheer lucency, Mind-as-such,
Whose actuality since its beginningness beginning,
    like the clear sky, has been a pure translucent
    continuity,
And whose supreme meaningfulness has remained
    unperturbed and inaccessible to propositions.

So that there may arise an understanding of the
    working of pristine cognitions which are the
    outcome of that intrinsic cognitive capacity within
    each of us,
Which is most wondrous Buddha intentionality,
Listen to my explanation of how I have experienced it
Through the elixir extracted from the essence of the
    Tantras, the discourses (by the Buddhas), and the
    instructions (by competent teachers).

In places pleasing to the mind in the four seasons,
Such as mountain peaks, dense forests, and islets,
A holistic feeling of calmness, well-focussed (on itself)
    and unperturbed,
Sheer lucency divested of all propositions about it will
    have to be cultivated.
And it will come through three factors concurring in
    natural purity:
Place, individual, and the content to be experienced.

BIb1   First, the place must be conducive to spiritual practices
        in the four seasons
By being secluded and enjoyable:
In summer, you should contemplate inside cool houses
        in cool places
Such as huts made of reeds or bamboo or fragrant grass
Near glaciers or mountain peaks.
In autumn, you should seasonally adjust your food,
        clothes, and activities
In houses and places where a balance is struck between
        cool and warm,
Such as dense forests and mountain slopes and
        rock-hewn dens.
In winter, you should adjust your food, clothing,
        bedding, and so on
In warm regions and low-lying places
Such as dense forests, mountain caves, and earthen
        houses.
In spring, it is most important that food, clothes, and
        activities are in harmony,
Whether you live in the mountains, forests, islets, or
In houses that are suitable in providing a balance
        between cool and warm.

Since the without and the within are the same in their
        hierarchical interaction,
You must resort to secluded and enjoyable places that
        are pleasing to the mind:
Since on mountain peaks the cognitive capacity clears
        and expands,
They are the places to dispel depression, and there the
        Developing Stage flourishes.
Since on glaciers holistic feeling becomes irradiating
        and lucent, and intrinsic awareness ever more clear,
They are the places to cultivate wider perspective, and
        there obstacles are few.

Since in dense forests, the cognitive capacity becomes
    settled in itself and stabilization of the mind
    takes place,
They are the places to cultivate inner calm,
    where a feeling of pleasure is very deep.
Near rocks, the awareness of impermanence and
    disgust with (what will not last) grows;
Clarity and sublimity grow more intense, and inner
    calm and wider perspective form a unity.
River banks make you attend to the essentials;
They quicken and renew the necessity to escape from
    the present situation.
Cremation grounds are a great blessing, and rewards
    (for spiritual efforts) come quickly.
They are said to be of highest value for realizing either
    the Developing Stage or the Fulfillment Stage.
Villages, markets, empty houses, solitary trees,
    and so on
Are places frequented by humans, non-humans,
    and goblins;
They are upsetting to the beginner and create obstacles,
But they are friends to those who are already firm and
    stable and hence are said to be of greatest value.
Shrine rooms, funeral monuments, and places with
    miasmic emanations[7]
Make your mind feel giddy and thoughts of
    hatred grow.
In places such as caverns with a languorous
    atmosphere[8]
Lust is born and feelings of depression and elation grow
    in excess.
Solitary trees having an aura of positive or negative
    afflatus,[9] as well as
Rocks and mountain spurs with their threatening
    dangers,[10]
Are said to make your mind feel giddy, to create

unfavorable conditions, and to set up many
obstacles.
Where outcasts, vicious snakes, and the deities of the
soil are living—
Lake shores, alpine meadows, dense forests,
Bedecked with lovely flowers and adorned with
fruit-bearing trees—
May, at first, be pleasing, but later on will create
many obstacles.

BIb2   In brief, there are places and houses which at first are
quite pleasing,
But the more familiar you become with them, they turn
out to be unpleasant with few rewards (for your
spiritual efforts);
There are others that at first are frightening and
vexatious, but become very pleasing the more
familiar you become with them;
They offer supreme blessings; rewards (for your
spiritual efforts) are quickly repeated, and there are
no obstacles.
Apart from these two kinds, all others are neutral and
do not offer any benefit or harm.

BIc   Since, depending on the place in which you reside, your
mind undergoes a change,
And there is either growth or decline in your efforts in
what is healthy and wholesome,
It has been said that it is of utmost importance to
examine the place or the locality.

To sum up, there are also four (kinds of) places
corresponding (in mood) to the four kinds of
actions:
Places inspiring 'inner calm' automatically keep the
mind steady;

Places conveying the feeling of 'expansion' have the
  mind rejoicing and resplendent in grandeur;
Places implying 'powerfulness' have the mind captured
  and attached;
Places conveying the feeling of 'severity' make the mind
  dizzy and induce dread and terror.
In their subdivision these places are countless and
  beyond measure.
Here, however, since places inspiring inner calm to aid
  holistic feelings are of primary importance,
The other places will not be discussed for fear of
  becoming too prolix.

In places inspiring inner calm, the meditation hut   BIIa
Must be set up in solitude so as to insure that the mind
  is kept steady;
The best type is one open at the sides and receiving
  plenty of light from above.

For meditation during the night, an absolutely dark   BIIb
  (and soundproof) room with an equally dark
  circumambulatory passage around it, is required,
The room itself being like the navel within the
  circumjacent structure situated on higher levels.
In this room you should lie down in the posture of the
  Buddha passing into Nirvāṇa, the pillow for the
  head turned northward.
During daytime the place for meditation should have
  much light:
Where the open sky can shine in and much light will
  come through the opening in the ceiling,
From glaciers, waterfalls, forests, and landscapes.
With the mind becoming radiant and pellucid,[11] a
  balance between cool and warm must be struck.

When the time has come to (attend to) inner calm, a   BIIc1
  solitary hut surrounded by a fence

Is the best place where stability of mind can grow
    naturally.

BIIc2   When the time has come to (attend to) wider
        perspective, much light and brightness from above
        is important.
It is important to have your mind continuously
    rejoicing and attuned to the seasons.

BIIc3   It is important to know these specifications:
Low-lying and shadowy areas such as forests and
    ravines are places for (developing) inner calm;
High localities such as snow-mountains and the like are
    places for (gaining) wider perspective.

C1   In brief, such localities as well as solitary huts—
Where the mind is kept to the essentials, escape from
    and disgust with (the present situation)—
Are the places where you should profitably apply
    yourself to what is healthy and wholesome since
    here holistic feelings grow.
Frequent them because they resemble the abode of
    limpid clearness and consummate perspicacity, the
    very quintessence (of life).

C2   But where, by living there, the healthy and wholesome
        diminishes and emotional disturbances increase,
And where worries about this life with all its
        excitements and distractions become overwhelming,
These are the places of spiritual death,[12] of evil deeds.
Hence, the wise will shun them.

C3   Since these places have been explained by
        Padmasambhava,
Those desiring liberation should know them.

CHAPTER TWO

The Individual

Man is not 'thrown into an alien world' but interacts with it in intricate ways which display a tendency towards order within us and around us. But there are also 'disordering' tendencies which, because they are or, at least, seem to be very powerful, have attracted wider attention. A more dispassionate view would see them as pointers to the overriding importance of the 'ordering' tendencies which are so conspicuous in living organisms. As a living organism, man, in particular, is an open, self-regulating system in non-equilibrium, not an immutable essence or closed system. Within his 'world' he struggles with himself in order to make himself 'whole'. But wholeness must not be misunderstood as implying that he has reached a terminus and now must stay put. This would reduce living man to a statistical and quantitative entity among other non-interacting closed systems.

Wholeness is qualitative and of paramount significance for man, that is, it constitutes a value worth striving for. Therefore, living man activates, on the reflective level of consciousness, error-correcting processes which are aimed at restoring him to his value from which he has moved away through misinterpretation of what is his goal. It is on this reflective level that a basically sound goal-directedness, as well as goal-informed striving, becomes distorted through misidentification. Inasmuch as value is intrinsic to the life of man, it functions effectively in it, as becomes evident from man's striving after goals (genuine or misconstrued ones). However, the full quality of value emerges only from a tension between opposites which must be resolved.

Living man is thus a complex dynamic pattern, not made up of isolated particular entities but of coordinated subpatterns which present an interdeterminate network of mutually qualifying causes and effects. As such a pattern or 'system', man appears as a process of adaptive self-organization and self-stabilization, by which the environment with which there is constant interaction is fitted to intrinsic constraints whereby the process organizes itself to a progressively more complex and 'efficient' pattern. This is to say, the adaptive self-organization is not 'merely' adaptive (utilitarian), but 'overflowing' ('creative' in the sense that man sees himself and his world with a fresh, life-enhancing vision), and the accompanying self-stabilization tends to maintain the resistance to perturbing forces in the environment.

Focussing on some of these qualitative processes and seeing them in the context of environment and growth, Klong-chen rab-'byams-pa illustrates the dynamic 'nature' of man as follows:

> Since confidence, perseverance, and the desire to escape are similar to a field whose nature is meaning, they are indispensable. Since disgust with Saṃsāra is the gate to meaning, it indicates the need to set out on the path towards deliverance. The concern with inner calm is similar to a seed (growing into) limpid clearness and consummate perspicacity. The impassionateness found in having dismissed from one's mind one's involvement in this lifetime becomes the

instrument of escaping from Saṃsāra. The desire for lasting limpid clearness and consummate perspicacity is like water and manure. Separation from excitements and emotional disturbances presents itself as the information that unfavorable conditions have been phased out by themselves. Visionary experiences and devotion are the spontaneously present cause for the increase of the crop that is the wholesome and healthy. Mental stability and a deep sense of reverence quickly ripen the fruit of the path towards deliverance. (A man in whom all this is taking place) is known as a most worthy vessel.[1]

To ensure the realization of the goal it becomes necessary to follow certain 'guide-lines' which seem, at first glance, to be suggested from outside, but which actually are already built into the 'system' presented by a human being, and effectively function in it. Such 'programs', which act like control centers, are known in anthropomorphic terms, as 'teacher', 'spiritual friend', and, going beyond this anthropomorphism, as 'the real Guru' (*bla-ma dam-pa*), who is none else but Mind-as-such (*sems-nyid*) which may be likened to an ever-present non-reflective input into the reflective level, the noetic-noematic complex (*sems*) which is but a manifestation or reflection and a condensation of the former.[2] The implication is that, at all times and simultaneously, there is at work a hierarchy of levels.

The hierarchical order of levels of dynamic processes by which a human existence ('system') becomes ever more richly orchestrated, is found, socially as well as spiritually, in the 'three constraints' or 'regulatory norms' that guide man to relate himself to a reality or world in whose shaping he is incessantly participating. These 'controls', 'norms', or 'constraints', seen in their social application, refer to the Śrāvaka who pursues a certain goal that remains strictly within the human dimensions of subjectivity; to the Bodhisattva whose goal takes in not only the world within him but also the one around him, particularly in interpersonal relationships; and to the mystic who attempts the short-cut of tuning in to the reality that embraces and goes beyond the human world:[3]

> A person who desires the Śrāvaka enlightenment abides by the constraints that go with the social types summed up by the term *prātimokṣa*;[4] he who desires unsurpassable Buddhahood to be realized within three or more aeons of countless years, trains himself in the constraints that mark a Bodhisattva; and he who desires Buddhahood quickly within his lifetime abides by the constraints that characterize the mystic way. These three disciplinary norms are termed 'foundation' because qualitatively they form a hierarchy while designatively and denotatively they are different.

But man is not just a social being; he is also a spiritual being bringing into play cognitions, insights, and interpretations, and there is interaction between his social and spiritual being. Viewed 'spiritually', the constraints operate as

> the constraint on the level of the *prātimokṣa*, that is, not to have the mind contaminated by emotional disturbances, the unhealthy and unwholesome; the constraint on the level of a Bodhisattva, which is to act on behalf of others in such a way that the healthy and wholesome is in a continual flow; and the constraint of the mystic, to have the bitendential value of Being (*don-gnyis*) spontaneously present by transfiguring oneself and the other (persons and the world) into deities and divine mansions, and to convert the reality values into the path of growing.[5]

The hierarchical order is such that the higher level constraints contain the lower level ones and, as is obvious, a lot more. Unless one's mind is kept free from emotional disturbances which distort our vision and make us see quantities where there should be (and actually are) qualities, it is not possible to recognize another person's value and act in such a way as to have this value kept alive. Unless one is able to perceive the value of Being, be it at first only in another person, it is not possible to be aware of one's own intrinsic values. Since this is not a state of invariance or conserved quantity, it operates in both directions: to the extent that I can see myself as valuable ('divine' or as a god or a goddess), I can see value in the world around me (others as gods or goddesses and the world itself as a divine mansion or a realm of exquisite beauty).

These levels or constraints do not apply to separate individuals, but operate in a single person moving in the direction of his real Being. Each person, taken separately, merely represents the actualization of any of the particular phases in this hierarchically ordering and ordered process. In other words, in view of the complexity of man, the 'three constraints' indicate applicable alternative patterns correlating with different sets of purposive acts by which a person defines himself as being of this or that type in face of a given challenge. The determination of which alternative should be applied in a situation which stimulates the application of constraint is a function of the particular competence of the individual. Inasmuch as these patterns are alike in setting up necessary restraints which are of a self-regulatory, goal-directed nature, there can never be any question of discarding restraints. Anyone irresponsible enough not to bother about the foundation of his growth will completely fail.

Lastly, growth starts in the person willing to grow by appreciating the uniqueness of his status as a human being. This is not ego conceit, because a person who can recognize himself as a human being also recognizes himself as part of a larger order. Precisely because he is 'subjective' he can also be 'objective', seeing value wherever it is. This the 'merely subjective' egotist is unable to do.

S econd, the person who is going to experience
for himself (life's meaning)
  Must be one who has confidence,[6] perseverance,
  the desire to escape (from his present situation) and
  the feeling of disgust (with it).
Wearied of Saṃsāra, he must deeply concern himself
  with liberation,
Dismissing this life from his mind and looking to
  limpid clearness and consummate perspicacity
  henceforward,[7]
Keeping excitement and distraction far away and
  having few emotions,
Being contented, leisurely, having visionary
  experiences, and being full of dedication,
Having a firm mind and a deep sense of reverence,[8]
[Such a person will realize most excellent liberation].[9]

He will have served, in the best possible way, a
  competent teacher,
And so have cultivated and refined his own mind by
  listening (to the words), thinking (about them), and
  making a living experience (of them), and,
In particular, he will spend day and night in
  continuous effort
To follow the instructions of what is the quintessence of
  the oral transmissions.
Not being distracted for a moment by trivialities,
He will strive for true individuality.

Not infringing the three status obligations of
The Śrāvaka, Bodhisattva, and mystic,[10]

He will control himself (so that) what is profitable to
    others will be realized,
And he will turn whatever appears into the path
    towards liberation.

B2   The beginner must primarily realize his own value:
In solitudes he must guard his mind, keeping
    excitement and distractions away;
Avoiding unfavorable conditions, he will have his
    emotions controlled by their counteragents.

B3   Not letting his vision and his actions contradict
    each other, he must pay attention to his
    contemplation and,
Tackling any of the five poisons that may arise within
    him, at that very moment,
By inspective attention, he must apply its counteragent
    directly.

B4   Conscientious about his actions by body, speech, and
    mind, and aware of them, having self-respect
And demonstrating decorum, he will refine himself.

B5   He has to be indifferent to praise or blame, approval or
    disapproval, fame or infamy,
These being but a phantom, a dream, with nothing
    to them.
He must contemplate them and accept them as if they
    were an echo,
And he must cut the mind, with its belief in an I or a
    Self, at its root.

B6   In brief, in not letting whatever he does contravene the
    meaning of life,
He must control himself and not harm others and,
Without for a moment giving in to the emotions,

It is imperative that he spends day and night in
    (applying himself to) what is healthy and
    wholesome.

Nowadays, in these evil times, it is most important   C1
That an unregenerate man realizes his own value in
    solitude.

Just as a bird with only one wing cannot rise into   C2
    the sky,
So without higher perception another's value cannot be
    perceived.
You must think about what is helpful to others by being
    cognizant of your own value.[11]

It is imperative that you realize (yourself) without   C3
    having your mind deceived
By the deception and trickeries perpetrated by Death
    (in the guise of) excitements and distractions.

Be not distressed by worries about when you might die.   C4

Therefore, you have to pin down mind today;   C5

Look where you would be carried away, if you were to   C6
    die today.

If you were to spend day and night in the welter of   C7
    excitements
Without having a hold on when you are going and what
    you are becoming,
Your being a unique occasion and the right juncture
    would be meaningless and a mere waste.
Alone and in solitude, contemplate what is meaningful.
Now is the time to take good counsel:

What will there be for me when I have to go at the
    moment of death?
Therefore, this very moment make efforts.

C8   The deceptive appearance of Saṃsāra resembles a
        frightening footpath.
Impress upon your mind the necessity to find a means
    to be delivered from it.
If you were to go astray now, you will go further and
    further astray in the future.
Therefore, exert yourself and take (this need) to heart.

C9   In the boat of a unique occasion and the right juncture,
        cross over the ocean of emotionality, the belief in a
        Self, which is so difficult to cross.

C10   Realize prosperity and bliss through efforts from your
        very heart,
While there is this rare opportunity of the road to
    liberation, the highway to limpid clearness and
    consummate perspicacity
Presenting itself through the power of your mind.

C11   Life is not permanent and changes every moment—
The wise (know that it is) vitiated by excitement and
    (only fools) postpone striving for what is healthy
    and wholesome.
When going astray has become the norm through one's
    having been accustomed to it for a long time,
The crowd of emotions turns up at every moment quite
    naturally.

C12   But since it is difficult for them to rise when you strive
        for merits and for what is wholesome,
It is imperative to strive to repel the motivating power
    of karmic actions.

In the realm of Saṃsāra there is no happiness   C13
    whatsoever;
If you think about the misery of fictitious being, it turns
    out to be unbearable.
Now you have to start with the means to liberation.

If you do not strive from the bottom of your heart for   C14
    life's meaningfulness,
There will be no profit in your having what makes you
    a unique occasion and the right juncture.
Therefore let your disgust with what is impermanent
    grow ever stronger,
And, not being distracted for a moment, put sustained
    effort into your realization.

Thus, if you have understood this from the first,   C15
The citadel of saintliness will afterwards be quickly
    reached.
Once your own value is established, that of others
    comes up naturally,
And the supreme path towards liberation from the
    realm of Saṃsāra is found.
Therefore, when whatever you do is in harmony with
    life's meaning,
You are an individual who has become the site for the
    realization of limpid clearness and consummate
    perspicacity.

CHAPTER THREE

The Experienced Content

Once the need for realization, deeply embedded in a living person (though not always responded to), has been felt, it seems to tend to make the person rush into this venture of finding himself. However, unless a proper foundation has been laid, the venture is bound to suffer shipwreck, often before the boat has even left harbor. It is for this reason, to avoid possible dangers, that the 'preliminaries' occupy such an important place in the process of growth, in what man must do in order to find himself through what may be called his real Being.

These 'preliminaries' present a hierarchical order of widening scope, already geared to bringing about the experience of a more satisfying reality. There is, first of all, the awareness of the transitoriness of life which impresses upon us the necessity to act now. Time is running out, and it is a mistaken belief that there may be a second chance. Transitoriness is not only observed around us as something that is just 'out there', but also applies to each of us and evokes the feeling of frustration culminating in disgust with all that is transitory and makes up our ordinary world. At the same time this feeling is the ever deepening knowledge that whatever is transitory cannot serve as a solid basis for shaping and finding meaning in life.

This knowledge is dialectically related to the manner in which we act in the face of the transitory. Action thus becomes compassion. Unlike activism with its inconsiderateness and disregard of responsibility, and unlike sentimentality with its hollowness and lack of genuine feeling, compassion as action (*thabs*) is dialectically related to the activation of the ethical impulse, which is 'value'-cognition (*shes-rab*) because of its being appreciative of the principles that govern human relationships as these progress to an optimum level. Still, there is a wide frame of reference. Action, which as the inner vitality of man is characterized and qualified as 'compassion,' becomes—in view of the ramifications in which it may manifest itself—a kind of 'experimenting', while 'appreciativeness', as its inseparable 'value'-cognition, frees us from the impasse or fixation into which 'action' alone might lead, and brings us up to higher levels of our being to which we refer as being states of meditation. This would not be possible without 'experimenting':

> Since without action appreciativeness is not born,
> At first search for meditative states by means of various
>   actions.[1]

'Action as compassion'—experimenting with more or less concrete situations—determines and defines. 'Appreciation', on the other hand, is not restricted to any one situation or appraisal but rather opens up the fixed framework. Their interaction, illustrated through the images of the masculine and feminine, guides one to 'act' in consonance with 'appreciation'. And the first instance of this interaction is the emergence of 'ethical man' who, in being aware of the value he himself constitutes and presents, becomes increasingly aware of the value of others which he concurrently strives to bring out. This can be done because, in value-cognition and value-oriented action, the dualistic separation between 'subject' (as an ego-encrusted isolation) and 'object' (as a statistically random plurality)—between one person and another, between men and women, between the masculine and feminine—is dissolved by one's understanding. This occurs through a growing kind of sensitivity and openness, the unity of the internal factors operating in the unfolding of what gradually has become one's dualistic world in and through which one is divided and suffers.

It is here that the 'empowerments' (*dbang*) fulfill an important role, inasmuch as they aid the person in re-discovering himself by clearing away the ego crust and opening up access to the inner creative forces. The English rendering, 'empowerment', refers to only one feature of the graded and complex process of man's deepening understanding of himself. The Tibetan term is understood as implying both 'catharsis' and 'empowerment'.[2] This ambiguity reflects the fact that the term refers to an experience of a unity which only on the reflective and descriptive level can be separated into two features. Furthermore, 'empowerment' is something like a 'forward' movement in linking up one level to the next higher one, so that by being in this process one also is the whole process. The important point to note is that all this is available within ourselves in the specific sense that 'within' is not merely the opposite to 'without', but that both 'within' and 'without' are merely surface phenomena that drag us further and further downward within something still deeper and more encompassing which defies any predication or reduction to something pre-established, be this in the manner of an essence or some other postulate. In other words, the 'empowerments' emerging out of the open dimension of Being operate through a context of encounters out of which, on the reflective level, holistic views of ourselves and our world arise with an ever increasing emphasis on quality and unity.

The 'Developing Stage' is initiated by the emerging quality—which is as much observed 'without' (in the external world) as it is felt 'within' (through the exercise of imagination)—as the application and execution of a plan, going beyond the 'obvious' in a creative way that is appropriate to the cultivation of man's very Being. Through this stage, the answers implicit to such questions as "Who am I?", "Where am I going?", "Why am I here?", are intimated, simply because insight has thus been gained into the difference between the state in which we are cut off from Being and the state in which we are attuned to Being. To see ourselves as a god or a goddess is not a deification of man (which merely reduces the intrinsic value of human beings), but is rather a recognition of the value of Being and a rediscovery of the creative forces that shape us.[3]

The 'Fulfillment Stage' is indicated by the unity of the within and the without which is felt, rather than judged propositionally—although to the reflective mind it presents itself as the paradox of there being something while there is nothing. This stage, being of a higher order, 'reaches down' into the lower order 'Developing Stage', and, with a shift of attention, both stages enter a new unity.

Actually, both stages are always together, and it is merely a matter of emphasis whether the 'experimenting' that goes with the Developing Stage or the 'appreciation' that is experienced in the Fulfillment Stage, is in the foreground. The path towards Being cannot be travelled in a one-sided manner. The internal logic is that there can be no 'appreciating' without 'experimenting'.

The 'preliminaries', then, open up communion with Being of which each of us is a presentation and which is encountered by each of us in specific ways. Although 'preliminaries', they are essential for the return to and rediscovery of that state that had been ours before we became alienated from ourselves by 'going astray' into worlds of frustration, where the 'light has gone out' and where we become more and more 'divided against ourselves'. However, these preliminaries are never an end in themselves.[4]

This 'state before'—to use a rather unusual index—is referred to by various terms such as 'self-existent pristine cognitiveness' (*rang-byung ye-shes*), 'pure awareness' (*rig-pa*), 'naturalness' (*gnyug-ma*), and 'togetherness' (*lhan-cig-skyes-pa*).[5] But these descriptive terms as well as their conceptual translations are faulty because the 'state before' is precisely one into which concepts (even that of 'state before') do not and never have entered. Therefore, no concept whatsoever can do justice to that which is actually involved. Even if we were to say that what is meant is the feeling of not being divided against oneself and the rest of the world, or of 'lighting up with joy', this is still to have recourse to concepts. Since we cannot do without concepts, all we can do is to be cautious not to confuse the concept with that to which it merely points:

> Although the fuel is not the fire itself, we can see it blaze forth from the fireplace; similarly, although the triad of pleasure (*bde*), radiance (*gsal*), and non-dividedness (*mi-rtog*) is not really this pure awareness, self-existent pristine cognitiveness, natural (mind), cognate (pristine cognition), it can be known by those who receive the Guru's instruction and who have the necessary devotion, from that which is indicated by 'bioenergetic level' which is pleasure, motility which is radiance, and the live structure (of flow-patterns) which is non-dividedness, (and which is taught) so that one may apply oneself to experimenting (with them).[6]

Although 'bioenergetic level' is essentially a term belonging to the realm of physiology and medicine, its use in this context is appropriate because it is equally the sustaining and creative force in personality from which health (even in the narrowest sense of the word as the state in which 'animal' functions are duly performed) and thought (in the wider sense of the capability to undo the perverted ego-limitations and restore the richness of man's 'inner' world) derive. It is, therefore, the same as the 'thrust towards Being'[7] which, quite literally, means to rediscover the optimal level of operation and which also is man's 'basic existence'[8] from which he is prone to alienate himself. This direct feeling of 'being'—what it is like to be fully awake, to be alone and yet to be all—is named after the feeling that accompanies the occurrences where we are at our best—'pleasure' (*bde-ba*). Therefore, pleasure is a mode of being perceived and known as a state of being fully alive and, as such, underlies any experience that we would claim to have a positive quality. However, as a judgment such a claim is already a limitation of the truly 'positive' character of pleasure or being, inasmuch as it has now become contrasted with 'negative'.

Closely related to pleasure is 'motility' (*rlung*) which carries waves of excitation which, although they are felt as 'pleasure', are also inputs of bioenergetic information. In being carried throughout the 'body', these inputs are being 'decoded', and it is here that 'something may go wrong', so that what may contribute to the overall well-being of the system becomes its restrictive and debilitating agency. This observation has led to the distinction between 'motility as the carrier of (and the movement informed by) pristine cognitiveness' (*ye-shes-kyi rlung*) and 'motility as the carrier of karmic activity' (*las-kyi rlung*) which is informed by 'mind' (*sems*) as ego-centered purposing.

> Although they are the same as far as movement is concerned, it is by virtue of movement along non-twisted conductors that motility becomes 'motility as the carrier of (and informed by) pristine cognitiveness', and it is known as such because its function is to display pleasure, openness, and radiance. But by moving along twisted conductors it becomes 'motility as the carrier of karmic activity'. Its function is the emergence of such deficiency experiences of motility as sundry dividing concepts, various unhealthy and unwholesome enjoyments, lack of radiance, depression, elation, obfuscation, and vertigo. As is the case with a changeling who

may, when infuriated, become a tiger, but if not, remains a human being, so also the effulgence of absolute cognitiveness ('informative input') and motility moving along the conductors in the body are identical; it is in view of the distortedness or non-distortedness of the conductors that it becomes the horse ('carrier') of pristine cognitiveness, the cognitive capacity operating appropriately, or of karmic activity and emotional imbalance, (the cognitive capacity) not operating appropriately.[9]

Motility, carrying waves of excitation and information, is observed outwardly, and felt inwardly, as 'radiance' (*gsal-ba*). To this we refer by saying that somebody 'shines with joy' or 'glows with pleasure'. This glow and radiance, the more intense it becomes, turns into sheer lucency, from which it originated in the concrete individual.

Motility is continuous with the patterns or conductors along which it flows. As such, these flow patterns exhibit a certain order that derives from 'within', in the sense elaborated above, and proceed from the non-manifest continuum towards increasingly discrete particulars. Their configuration represents a system of a highly complex, self-organizing and self-manifesting kind. These particulars, known technically as 'conductors', 'flow-patterns', 'circuits' (*rtsa*) are to be understood as functionally, not representationally, true and relevant to the subject as a live person who is constantly 'decoding' the messages that are sent out. As has been pointed out earlier, in this 'decoding' process conflicting features may enter, which eventually lead to emotional imbalance in and cognitive distortion of the continuum of Being, of which the living person is a concrete presentation. 'Non-dividedness' (*mi-rtog-pa*) is but the connectivity of the 'flow-pattern system', which is both 'knowing' and 'known' in a non-partitive manner to which we refer as being 'beyond subject and object'.

Pleasure, radiance, and non-dividedness are 'facts' as they are perceived and interpreted by cognizant human individuals, but they are also 'values' inasmuch as they are made dynamic qualities of the cognizant human individual. This emphasis on 'lived values' is central to what is meant by 'meditation'.

Two tendencies, however, seem to operate in every living organism which, as has been noted, is characterized by a constant openness of its boundaries which makes the operation of these tendencies possible. One tendency which is of primary importance develops towards higher levels of organization involving optimal value states by making use of negentropic input. This tendency is furthered by 'meditation' as a means of 'tuning in' to the openness of Being. The other tendency is 'entropic' and develops towards a final state of rest or death. The entropic character of this tendency is inherent in the sense that this process becomes ever more statistically repetitive. In terms of the reflective ego, this means that we may try to pursue intrinsically value-optimizing facets of Being (such as pleasure) which we have nonetheless consciously misapprehended by seeing them 'out of context' and as an 'end in themselves' and of which we consequently engage in repeat performances (that are also euphemistically called 'meditation'). Alternatively, we may merely descend into and persist in a state of random fluctuation and ultimate disorderliness. However, precisely because of the fact that living organisms are open systems —and man is no exception—there is always present and operative the other trend towards higher levels of organization. To make use of it is to mend our deficiency which, rather than being an inescapable 'state of fallenness', is a challenge strictly within ourselves.

A   **T**hird, there are three steps concerning that which
         is to be experienced:
         The preliminaries, the main body, and the
       summary.

AI   First, the preliminaries will be shown:

AIa   Awareness of transitoriness and disgust with Saṃsāra
        are the external preliminaries;
    They thoroughly dispel the preoccupation with this life.

AIb   Compassion and the activation of the ethical impulse
        are the special preliminary;
    They make everything travel along the path of the
        Mahāyāna.
    Therefore, at the beginning, cultivate these two
        preliminaries.

AII   After them come the most sublime preliminaries:

AIIa The exercise of the Two Stages,[10] after having received
        the empowerments in full;
    When one (experiences) one's own body transfigured as
        a god and the world and its beings as gods
        (and palaces),
    The involvement in vulgar beliefs is dispelled.

AIIb When one cultivates the profound path, the
        communion with the Guru,
    Immeasurable waves of spiritual sustenance arise from
        the power of compassion.

All hindrances are removed and the two kinds of
    rewards (for one's spiritual efforts) are obtained.
Therefore, the two sublime preliminaries have to be
    cultivated.

Thus by these four topics making up the preliminaries,   AIII
Mind is set on the unerring path, and,
The sublime path towards liberation having been taken
    hold of, the experience of Being comes quickly.
It becomes easy to cultivate the main features (of what
    is to be experienced), there are no obstacles, and
There are capabilities without limits such as coming
    ever closer to the rewards (of one's spiritual efforts).
Therefore it is of utmost importance to cultivate the
    preliminaries.

The main body is about 'pure awareness', encountered   B
In the experience of Being by means of 'meditation'
    involving pleasure, radiance, and non-dividedness.
As sheer lucency, a pristine cognitiveness, defying any
    propositions about it,
It rises in naturalness and togetherness.

First, there is the encounter by means of 'pure pleasure':   BIa
After you have pursued the preliminaries as indicated
    above,[11]
(You have to imagine) three 'conductors' in the manner
    of three pillars in the midst of four 'control centers';
The 'conductor' to the right is white, the one to the left
    red, and the central one deep blue.
Its upper end extends to the cranium, its lower end to
    the perineum.
Within the central 'conductor' directly in front of the
    'navel' region, there comes from its syllabic
    symbol A
A blazing fire that makes 'nectar'[12] flow down from the
    syllabic symbol HAM in the head.

This nectar fills all the four central centers and the
    whole body.
When the feeling of pleasure becomes pervasive, there
    flows down to the syllabic symbol vaṃ in the heart
    region
The 'nectar' of the haṃ in an incessant stream.
This one has to cultivate until the experience of
    ‘pleasure has set in.
Then even the vaṃ becomes smaller and smaller, and
    subtler and subtler,
And (finally) settles in a field (of feeling) that defies any
    propositions as to its three kinds of objective
    reference (i.e., a—haṃ—vaṃ).
When by this means the mind has been taken hold of,
    there comes an inner calm through pleasure.

B1b   After this, the mind, having passed beyond whatever
    can be thought or talked about,
Rises as this field that is similar to the (clear) sky, free
    from the intellect's ruminations.
This is sheer lucency, complete and perfect as pure
    pleasure and openness,
Meaningfulness that in its pellucidity cannot be
    encompassed by ordinary thought.[13]

B1c   Once you have become familiar with it, there come four
    experiences:
Everything that is presented (to the mind) is (felt) to rise
    in pleasure;
Day and night, you cannot be torn from this reach and
    range of pleasure;
Tribulations like attachment and aversion do not
    upset you;
There is born an appreciative understanding that brings
    together words and meanings;
By further cultivating this there rise, like the sun, in
    your mind,

Unfathomable capabilities such as visions and higher
    cognitions.
This, then, is instruction in the most profound.

Second, there is the encounter by means of 'radiance':   BIIa
The preliminaries are as before, by imagining how at
    their lower end the right and left conductors,
That have been made to glow, enter the central
    conductor;
And how their upper ends enter the nostrils, and then
By blowing out (through them) the waste from 'motility'
    three times, the demons of disease and the
    obscurations by evil disperse.
Drawing in the breath slowly three times, (you have to
    imagine) the whole world (stationary and moving),
    (first)
To dissolve in a pure light, which is then drawn into
    your self through the nose, and which
Enters the central conductor from those to its right and
    left; and (then imagine) the pure light to settle in the
    center of the heart in the hues (of the five pristine
    cognitions), and finally
To dissolve in a globule (of light).
Holding (this light) as long as you can,
You should take a little time to discharge the union of
    the upward and downward trends of motility.
It is most important that inhaling and exhaling are
    done slowly.
Moreover, you must not let the capabilities such as
    those inherent in (this emergent) Buddhahood
Become dispersed into any place, but you should let
    them dissolve in the heart.
By this means the mind is steadied in its radiance
    and pellucidity.

Thereafter, you have to imagine how the light from the   BIIb
    heart's light

Encompasses the whole universe by its outward
    spreading
Which starts from the blaze within the four control
    centers within the body.
When you practice this day and night for some time,
Dreams cease and manifestations of light set in,
And you see the within and the without engulfed in a
    light of five colors,
Which (come in intensities of) the rising moon, a
    shining lamp, a firefly, a star, and so on.
When the mind is firmly settled in this range of
    radiance, inner calm is born.

BIIc   Then when you gather in the light again and let even
    the light of the heart
Become smaller and smaller and subtler and subtler in
    the reach and range of openness,
There rises mind in radiance and pellucidity and
    openness with no referential point whatsoever in it,
As sheer lucency that in itself is free from any
    limitations by propositions about it.

BIId   This is natural pristine cognitiveness in its radiance
    and openness;
It is the experience of Being in its natural completeness.
Once you have become accustomed to it there come
    four experiences:
Whatever is presented (to the mind) is felt to be a
    shimmering, wide-open lucency;
Day and night you stay in this range of radiance;
Mind in its radiance and pellucidity is not upset by
    dividing concepts;
And there is an appreciative awareness that is
    expanding without noematic-noetic interference.

BIIe   Further, by becoming accustomed to it, there arise
    these capabilities:

To see clearly what lies behind the screen, as well as
To have higher experiences.
This is the essence of a still profounder instruction.

Third, the encounter by means of 'non-dividedness':　　BIIIa
The preliminaries are as before; the main procedure has
　　three facets:
Projecting, fixing, refining.
'Projecting' means to let the sheer lucency which is
　　Mind-as-such,
Like (the syllabic symbol) A or a globule of (five-colored
　　light) in the heart,
Depart from your head far up into the sky
As you vigorously exclaim 'HA' twenty-one times.
The moment body and mind become thoroughly
　　relaxed and composed
In the range which becomes ultimately invisible, the
　　higher the projection is effected, and
The flow of divisive concepts is stopped.
You stay in a range that cannot be expressed in words,
　　however much you might try;
Even its experience is such that nothing is to be seen (as
　　something), passing beyond the reach of thought.

'Fixing' is to turn your back to the sun　　BIIb
And steadily gaze at the clear sky;
And when, unnoticeably, the movement of 'motility'
　　becomes calmer and calmer,
Non-dividedness, defying any propositions, wells up
　　from deep within,
And an experience as open as the sky is born naturally.

'Refining' means, while keeping the eyes steadily fixed　　BIIIc
　　on the sky,[14]
To imagine how out of the range in which mind is
　　radiant, neither forging ahead nor withdrawing,

Earth, stones, mountains, rocks, and the whole animate
 and inanimate world
Becomes one with the wide open sky.
Your own body is felt to be without grosser matter,
Mind and sky are in a state of indivisibility, and
There is no stirring of the without, within, or
 in-between.
When body and mind have relaxed in this range
 of the sky,
There is this reach and range in which subjective
 thinking with its attending and intending has
 become calm;
Let mind, no longer forging ahead nor withdrawing,
 settle in its place.
At that time meaningfulness, mind beyond words
 and thoughts,
Arises as (ultimate) intentionality like the sky,
 non-dual;
This is the very essence of all the Buddhas of the
 three times.

BIIId Once you have become accustomed to this there are
  four experiences:
Whatever is presented (to the mind) is free-flowing,
 there being no gross conceptual articulations;
Day and night you cannot be separated from this range
 of non-dividedness;
The five poisons[15] have become calm by themselves
 and the mind's stream is gentle and mild;
There is the felt experience of everything being
 like the sky.

BIIIe Once you have thus become accustomed to
  non-dividedness as the third means,
Wider visions, higher cognitions, holistic feeling, and
 (Buddhahood) capabilities set in,

Appropriate action and appreciative discrimination,
    inner calm and wider perspective enter into a unity,
And through them, incidentally as well as ultimately,
    the most excellent bitendential value of Being is
    realized.

In the summary there are four sections: C
The experience itself, bringing out its worth, its
    understanding, and the climax.

From among the two kinds of experience, the one   CIa
    without flaws has been discussed above.

The one with flaws derives from compulsive addiction   CIb
    to each of (its) three facets:
Addiction to 'pleasure', to 'radiance', and to
    'non-dividedness';
Compulsive addiction to (each) as an end in itself, their
    reversal, and their being mixed with 'poison' are
    their three flaws.[16]

Reversal of 'pleasure' involves a drop in the   CIci
    bioenergetic level, libidinous urgings taking
    precedence,
A feeling of discontent, listlessness, and the desire to
    think in terms of objectification.

Reversal of 'radiance' is increase in palpitation,   CIcii
    prevalence of irritation-aversion,
A hardening of divisive concepts, perplexity, and
    reluctance to be at rest.

Reversal of 'non-dividedness' is dullness and   CIciii
    lusterlessness, and
Mind becomes depressed, drowsy, sluggish, and
    inarticulate.

Thus one has to tackle any deficiency, whether it is due
    to an inherent propensity or downright entropic,
And to mend it by means of the appropriate
    counteragent.[17]

CI   To bring out the full worth (of the experience), one has
    to mend its deficiency and deepen the experience.

CIIa1   There are three ways of mending the deficiency:
A person (of highest intelligence) does so by insight:
He knows all that is postulated by the intellect to be
    like an apparition,[18] having no essence whatsoever
    that could be grasped;
To be like the one overarching sky, to have nothing to
    boast of, and to be nothing by themselves;
And he passes the verdict on them that they are of the
    sphere where no compulsive addiction obtains.
Pitfalls and obscurations become the experience of
    Being;
Obstacles spur him on toward what is healthy and
    wholesome, and unfavorable conditions aid him to
    limpid clearness and consummate perspicacity;
On the ground that is pure pleasure, his mind
    (operates) constantly in a state of pleasure,
And an understanding comes that is like the sky
    unlimited.

CIIa2   A person of mediocre intelligence mends (the
    deficiency) by contemplation and bringing out
    (the mind's) pellucidity.
He catches (it as in a snare) and holds it by attentive
    inspection,
And installs it in the sphere of 'pleasure', 'radiance',
    and 'non-dividedness' where there is no distraction.
Since distraction, and the failure to catch it, are a defect,
It is imperative to have (the mind) every moment in the
    reach and range where no distractions occur.

When there is a reversal of pleasure he should CIIa2i
   imagine that
A blazing fire starting from the ʜᴜᴍ in the 'energy
   reservoir'[19] consumes all grossness in his body
And cleanses and transports him into the range where
   there is nothing concrete.
This procedure applies also to cases of illness and
   obsession.
Having broken the clinging to 'pleasure', he should
   contemplate 'pleasure' as an open dimension.
As he increasingly scrutinizes the mind in which
   libidinous urgings stir, it is then,
When this mind is installed in the sphere where neither
   hope nor fear nor anything contrived or adulterated
   exists, that
Libidinous urgings are resolved by themselves, and a
   pristine cognition that is pure pleasure and
   openness (together) arises.
Discontent is a defect that comes with a decrease in
   'bioenergetic input';
(Against it) he should contemplate a 'setting' which is
   felt as 'pleasure' flowing (because its frozen state has
   been thawed) by a blazing fire.
If there is deep depression, this is the fault of
   condensation not having been separated from
   radiation.
(Against it) he has to straighten his body,
Start deep breathing and filling the heart with 'light'.
By contemplating the world of appearances as well as
   the ideas about it as filled with light and as
   radiance-openness, (depression) is resolved.

In order to weaken the clinging to 'radiance' he has to CIIa2ii
   practice absolute non-subjectivity.
When there is the reversal of 'radiance', that is,
   lusterlessness, he has to contemplate mind as
   pellucid and radiant.

When there is rapid palpitation or restlessness (of the
    mind), he should close his eyes and in his heart
Contemplate lucency or a syllabic sound symbol or a
    lotus, a sword, a cross,
And should let any of them, the lower these descend,
    the farther extend
Until they hit the golden layer below.[20]
This is the surest way of dispelling (the reversal).
When the prevalence of irritation-aversion is contained
    in its own course,
It will dissolve in the mirror-like pristine cognition that
    is radiance-openness.

IIa2iii   The rising of 'non-dividedness' is practiced by
    non-subjectivity.
When the mind, on its threshold to dullness, is
    recognized as what it is and scrutinized,
It dissolves at that very moment, and a pristine
    cognitiveness which is the continuum of
    meaning arises.
When there is listlessness, sluggishness, and
    inarticulateness,
He should contemplate the light in his heart as it comes
    out of the crown of his head
And remains hovering in the sky above him.
When the mind is held there, it stays divorced from all
    propositions.
This is the instruction in the most profound topic.

In general, non-subjectivity is of utmost significance in each
    and every case.
If there is no longer hope or fear, you are free from all
    hindrances.
When Mind-as-such, openness and lucency, is installed in
    (its) sphere of pellucidity,
Divested from the propositions about it, which are the
    concretization of the intellect,

You are certainly free from spiritual obstacles and do not
   travel wrong ways to be avoided.

Those of low intelligence in mending the deficiencies   CIIa3
Resort to three procedures: postures, diet, sympathetic
   magic.
Posture involves the seven items of the
   Vairocanābhisambodhi:[21]
Sitting cross-legged, with a fixed stare, breathing
   calmly,
Holding the hands folded, bending the neck slightly,
   raising the tongue to the palate,
Lowering the eyes to the tip of the nose, and (thereby)
   harmonizing 'motility' and 'mentation'.
There being neither depression nor elation, an unfailing
   concentrative 'setting' is born.
Since all defects arise from the body's vitalizing forces
   being upset, that is,
The 'conductors', the 'motility', and the 'bioenergetic
   input' being disturbed,
It is important to remain in a state of composure in
   which upsetting disturbances do not enter.
And since capabilities, in turn, arise when the
   'conductors', 'motility', and 'bioenergetic input'
Have become the vitalizing forces without interference,
It is important to scrutinize these vitalizing forces.

From among other similar body exercises,
In particular, slowness, gentleness, and tranquillity are
   very important.
A person has to temper gentleness with impetuosity
   and impetuosity with gentleness.
And it is of utmost importance to have all that is
   involved suited to his temperament.
Specifically, with respect to 'pleasure' he must cross
   his arms,

Lower his eyes, and hold the mind on 'pleasure'.
With respect to 'radiance' he must lay his hands on
      his knees,
Breathe slowly, and stare at the sky.
As for 'non-dividedness', this is achieved by the seven
      items (mentioned above).

Diet means to rely on what is beneficial to the
      experiences such as food and drink
At places suited to the seasons and in company.

Sympathetic magic is to preserve one's bioenergetic
      level by tying round one's waist
A charmed cord that consists of three threads woven
By a virgin, in case of a drop in the bioenergetic level.
When there is a rush of dividing concepts,
      non-dividedness is established
By using a pill made of sandal, saffron, and excreta;
And when there is dullness, holistic feelings are assured
By pills of saffron, camphor, and 'hormones', so a
      Tantra says.[22]

If a person is to deepen the flawless experience of
      'pleasure', 'radiance' and 'non-dividedness',
The best thing to do is to keep the mind to any
      objective reference.
First, he has to contemplate while depending on the
      objective reference;
Thereafter he moves automatically into the
      non-referential range.
Since this is the most profound and sublime procedure,
The fortunate one must comply with it.
To dismiss it because it starts with a specific
      characteristic is the way of fools;
Theirs is to be dismissed as a bad method as no
      experience whatever is ever felt (to arise).

In particular, to bring out the real value of 'pleasure',   CIIb1
He has to stop the downward movement of 'motility'
    and to have it fade upwards in the bioenergetic
    input, starting from the perineum
And dissolving in the crown of the cranium,
And then to install (this feeling) in the reach and range
    where there is no objective reference.
Afterwards when the union of the downward and
    upward movements has been taken hold of
And the mind, concentrated on the heart, becomes
    installed in the sphere where there is no origination
    of (subjective thoughts),
This is the presence of 'pleasure' and 'radiance'
    divorced from all propositions about it.[23]

From time to time the person should watch this 'energy
    movement'
(Assuming the forms of) a descent, a turn-about or a
    pulling up, dispersal, and a finalizing,
Like the lithe shaking of a lion.

'Descent' is like his raising the upper part of his body
    and pressing down the lower one
In the union with his imaginary consort in embrace,
By pulling the 'creative energy' from the HAṀ
And letting it descend into the genital region he fixes
    the mind on 'pleasure'.

'Turn-about' is to pull this downwards movement
    upwards:
He places both hands on the groin,
While pulling up the downward movement the tongue
    is made to touch the palate;
The white in the eye is turned up and, with neck and
    head quivering,
He imagines the bioenergetic input, like a tightened
    rope (being pulled in), to

Fade in one vital spot after the other, up to the crown of
the head.

'Dispersal' is agility of hands and feet (as in) preparing
bow and arrow for shooting;
The breath is let out with a hissing sound, the tip of the
tongue touching the teeth.

'Finalizing' is to lie supine and be completely relaxed;
Not to entertain any concepts nor to hold to anything,
And to be in a state where no propositions naturally
obtain.
Thereby limpid clearness and consummate perspicacity
which is pure pleasure without any impediments is
set up.[24]

CIIb2   When one brings out the value of 'radiance' (related to)
'motility',
The one, as for instance, gentle movement, is to bring
out the other, as for instance, harshness;
In particular, in the interaction between the within and
the without,
It is important that slowness and gentleness fuse.
Although it has been said that many techniques have to
be studied,
Such as counting (the rate of breathing), the color, the
temperature, and the shapes (breath may assume),
(They are of no avail).[25]
The technique used here, where everything is achieved
by a simple procedure,
Is the king among the essences in the instructions.

When you have brought the body into the posture as
discussed before, and, in particular, when there is
no longer any eye movement,
Breathing must proceed very slowly through the mouth
and the nostrils,

And you must easily relax in the state of genuine
   freedom.
Mind must be made not to grasp anything.
Afterwards you have to lie supine, arms and legs
   stretched,
And, with a vigorous 'HA', to let the mind rise
   to the sky,
And let it stay in its own luster without any distractions,
   there being neither a forging ahead to, nor
   withdrawal from, (its 'objects').
When 'motility' and 'mentation' are in a state of
   'pleasure' that is free in itself,
There are no obstacles, and there are infinite openings
   for capabilities to arise.

The body feels light and no breathing movement is
   sensed; all propositions have come to rest, and
Mind is radiant and pellucid and higher cognitions
   arise.
You can move with lightning speed, your complexion is
   shining, and holistic feelings grow.
There comes the indication that 'motility' and
   'mentation' have entered the 'center'.
This most profound and sublime feature is a great
   secret.

Also, in bringing out the value of 'non-dividedness'   CIIb3
   which is like the sky,
Body and mind must be relaxed, and concentration
   must be on one topic.
The longer you look at this one topic in an undistracted
   manner,
All other divisive thought-constructs disappear in it.
When, even with respect to this topic, thoughts have
   fully ceased,
There comes an openness that does not hold what is
   present to be this or that.

This is the main point.

Moreover, the following, too, has to be learned:

Sometimes 'non-dividedness' is born from the
'without',

As when breath is exhaled and becomes the objective
reference;

Sometimes it does so when, in a state of
undistractedness, the objective reference

Is either within, or above, or below.

Sometimes it is born when the cognitive capacity has
nothing to rest on

And stays in a state where there is no concretization of
what appears to be(come) an object.

This is 'non-dividedness' or the intentionality of the
founding stratum of meaning.

It comes by itself deep out of itself when this technique
is used.

In order to bring out the real value of pleasure,
radiance, and non-dividedness, it is said that

The accumulation of merits and knowledge, the
removal of the intellectual and emotional
obscurations, the attention to the Developing and
Fulfillment Stages,

And the profound path, the communion with the real
teacher, are the most excellent procedures.

This is the instruction on the ultimate quintessence.

Those fortunate ones desirous of liberation must take it
to heart.

CIII The understanding (of Being) that comes, when you
have contemplated in this way,

Has one flavor that remains the same, as there is neither
differentiation nor plurality in it.

This one place in which the three approaches converge

Is like the ocean into which the various rivers flow.

Whichever approach of the three, 'pleasure', 'radiance',
or 'non-dividedness' you may have practiced,
When the operations of the intellect have become quiet
and subsided
In what is like the sky, unborn, Mind-as-such,
It is this very thrust towards limpid clearness and
consummate perspicacity divorced from the
propositions about its existence or non-existence,
That rises out of the depth (of Being) as sheer lucency,
the sun of Being itself;
This is an understanding that need not be affirmed nor
negated and that does not step out of itself, nor turn
into something other than itself.
It is the very thrust of vitalizing (Buddhahood) which,
like the sky, remains the same.

At that time, in the ocean of concentration in which
inner calm and wider perspective spread
And which is well-focussed (on itself), pellucid and
radiant without any turbidness,
All images, unlimited, without subjective distortion, are
nothing as such
And enter into unity with the very facticity of the
understanding of all and everything.
Whatever appears is like an apparition, nothing (in its
ever felt presence), and not held to be this or that.
This vast intentionality, whose unity cannot be split,
Is sheer lucency that, originating from this facticity,
comes out of the depth of (its) Being.

This self-existing pristine cognitiveness, (evoked
through) the Guru's sustaining power,
Is seen when words and thoughts and talk have
passed away.
To see it then as time

Is (the moment) when the three aspects of time are
    no-time, and a 'before' or a 'later' can no longer be
    distinguished.
It is called Prajñāpāramitā, Mādhyamika,
Zhi-byed, calming (the rush of) propositions and
    suffering,[26] Mahāmudrā,
rDzogs-chen, the very meaningfulness of
    meaningfulness.
It is the experience of Being from its beginningless
    beginning, in
Sheer lucency, Mind-as-such, self-existent pristine
    cognitiveness.
Although it may be given many names, it remains the
    one pure fact of Being as value,
Meaningfulness, defying words and thoughts about it,
    and mind as limpid clearness and consummate
    perspicacity.
Like the sky, where neither Saṃsāra nor Nirvāṇa exist
    as something in a framework of duality,
This absolute completeness—in its remaining the same,
    non-dual, divorced from the intellect,
Impartial, beyond the jungle of philosophical systems—
The yogis must know thoroughly
As the vast, unlimited Buddha intentionality.

CIV   The gradation in the climax, once the above have
        reached their ultimate limits, is
    That, incidentally, through the unity of 'pleasure',
        'radiance', and 'non-dividedness',
    There come illimitable capabilities such as wider vision
        and higher cognitions,
    And that, ultimately, Buddhahood (exemplified by) the
        three founding strata of meaning is realized like a
        Wish-fulfilling Gem so that
    The bitendential value of Being is spontaneously
        present.

When, through the merits of having explained in depth
and width
The very meaning of life, the meaningful inner calm,
The two facets of limpid clearness and consummate
perspicacity have been realized,
May infinite wealth accrue through the activity of the
Wish-fulfilling Gem.

The above has been compiled according to his own
experience
By the Buddhist Dri-med 'od-zer,
And for the benefit of future generations this clear
presentation
Has been written down in Gangs-ri thod-dkar, an
ornament of the mountains.

May those desirous of gaining freedom make every
effort
And have an experience as stated here.
When the most excellent value of Being will have been
realized by them, for the time being and ultimately,
They will quickly rejoice and be happy in the island of
Pure Pleasure.

Notes

Notes to Introduction

1) 'Buddha intentionality' (*sangs-rgyas-kyi dgongs-pa*) is a key term in rDzogs-chen thought. On the meaning of *sangs-rgyas*, see *Kindly Bent to Ease Us*, part 1, p. 256 n.17, 274 n.3, and on that of *dgongs-pa*, Ibid., p. 261 n.6. Both terms are 'descriptive' of *rig-pa* which has been rendered by 'pure awareness', but it implies much more than a mere cognitive process. It points to the whole life process which is even greater than life itself. If *rig-pa* is seen dynamically as the input or inflow of energy in an open system (as is suggested by the term *sangs-rgyas* which could well be associated with the idea of 'order through fluctuation'; see Erich Jantsch, *Design for Evolution*, p. 37 and *passim*) then *dgongs-pa* points to purpose and order and meaning in life. Such meaning reverberates in the various 'founding strata' (*sku*) for the various 'founded cognitions' (*ye-shes*). See *Lung-gi gter-mdzod*, 65ab.

2) *Lung-gi gter-mdzod*, 20a f.

3) Ibid., 20b–21b.

4) This is the *Yi-ge med-pa'i rgyud chen-po* (in *rNying-ma rgyud-'bum*, vol. 9, p. 366; *rNying-ma'i rgyud bcu-bdun*, vol. 2, p. 220).

5) This is the *Chos thams-cad rdzogs-pa chen-po byang-chub-kyi sems kun-byed rgyal-po* (in *rNying-ma rgyud-'bum*, vol. 1, p. 145).

6) Ibid., p. 146.

7) *Theg-pa'i mchog rin-po-che'i mdzod*, II, p. 84. *gSang-ba bla-na-med-pa 'od-gsal rdo-rje snying-po'i gnas-gsum gsal-bar byed-pa'i tshig-don rin-po-che'i mdzod*, p. 216. This text will hereafter be quoted in its abbreviated form of *Tshig-don rin-po-che'i mdzod*.

8) *Tshig-don rin-po-che'i mdzod*, p. 216.

9) The term 'evolutionary' is used in the sense elaborated by Erich Jantsch, *Design for Evolution*, p. 35 and *passim*.

10) In *rNying-ma rgyud-'bum*, vol. 9, p. 412; *rNying-ma'i rgyud bcu-bdun*, vol. 3, pp. 198 f. Also quoted in *Tshig-don rin-po-che'i mdzod*, p. 214, and *Theg-pa'i mchog rin-po-che'i mdzod*, II, p. 75.

11) In *rNying-ma rgyud-'bum*, vol. 10, p. 14. Also quoted in *Tshig-don rin-po-che'i mdzod*, p. 215.

12) In *rNying-ma rgyud-'bum*, vol. 10, pp. 17–18.

13) *Theg-pa'i mchog rin-po-che'i mdzod*, II, pp. 76, 78, 79; *Tshig-don rin-po-che'i mdzod*, p. 228.

14) In *rNying-ma rgyud-'bum*, vol. 10, p. 17; *Theg-pa'i mchog rin-po-che'i mdzod*, II, p. 83; *Tshig-don rin-po-che'i mdzod*, p. 227.

15) In *rNying-ma rgyud-'bum*, vol. 10, p. 17; *Theg-pa'i mchog rin-po-che'i mdzod*, II, p. 83; *Tshig-don rin-po-che'i mdzod*, p. 216.

16) Klong-chen rab-'byams-pa discusses this point in his *Tshig-don rin-po-che'i mdzod*, pp. 217 f, in connection with the aids to implementing this 'setting'. Generally speaking, thoughts about solid food are dismissed as one learns to live more and more on 'spiritual' food. See also *Theg-pa'i mchog rin-po-che'i mdzod*, I, p. 503.

17) *mKha'-gro snying-thig*, part 2, p. 51. The Tibetan term translated by 'bioenergetic input' (*thig-le*) comprises both the 'physical' and the 'psychic', if not even more. In his *Theg-pa'i mchog rin-po-che'i mdzod*, II, p. 365, Klong-chen rab-'byams-pa defines *thig-le* as follows: "*thig* means 'unchanging' ('unalterable') and *le*

'all-encompassing by virtue of its spreading far and wide'," and he distinguishes different operations by it, all of which occur in a continuum. With reference to the living body, *thig-le* is similar to what we call the 'genetic code' and its presence in every single cell. In the same work, I, p. 573, Klong-chen rab-'byams-pa gives a further definition of *thig-le* as "surrounded by orbiting bands of five light values, radiant in themselves, a pellucid color (spectrum)." Both definitions taken together suggest the idea of an atom with its nucleus and orbiting electrons, the electrons being represented by (a) the orbiting light values, and the nucleus by (b) the energy of the orbiting values (intensities) as a constant. But it is also possible to think of *thig-le* as a 'code' and, since the dynamic aspect is so prominent, as a continual 'coding'. This input is then processed by 'appreciation' (*shes-rab*), which decides what is to be done with the information pouring in; and 'action' (*thabs*) then works out the 'problem', providing, as it were, the practical answer. The association of 'radiance' (*gsal-ba*) with 'action' is something like a process display device that shows 'how things are going', while 'pleasure' (*bde-ba*) related to 'appreciation' indicates the state of satisfaction with the uninterrupted 'input'. The definition of *thig-le* as 'unchanging' does not refer to something entitatively given, but to an utter 'openness'. See *Rig-pa rang-shar chen-po'i rgyud* (in *rNying-ma rgyud-'bum*, vol. 10), pp. 206 f.

18) Ibid., p. 61.

19) *mKha'-'gro yang-thig*, part 2, p. 172.

20) This is not to say that there are not more than four control centers. The number actually depends on which 'model' is under consideration. In *mKha'-'gro yang-thig*, part 2, pp. 192 f, Klong-chen rab-'byams-pa discusses from one to six control centers. Similarly, there is an infinite number of 'conductors' which in their interconnections act like self-reinforcing and self-maintaining loops, representing functional regularities, but only three or four are singled out for detailed discussion.

21) *Theg-pa'i mchog rin-po-che'i mdzod*, I, p. 487.

22) *Theg pa'i mchog rin po che'i mdzod*, I, p. 507; *mKha'-'gro yang-thig*, part 2, p. 155. In this work, on p. 156, Klong-chen rab-

'byams-pa mentions a fifth 'control center' in the posterior end of the central axis (the pelvic region or perineum), termed *bde-skyong-gi 'khor-lo*, 'pleasure preserving control center'. As the name implies it seems to have to do with maintaining the needed constancy of the organism's interaction with the environment (internal and external). The required norm, here called 'pleasure', would then correspond to our concept of homeostasis. But since everywhere dynamic processes are involved, it might be more appropriate to speak of homeorhesis, a term coined by C. H. Waddington. See on this problem Erich Jantsch, *Design for Evolution*, p. 92 note.

23) *Theg-pa'i mchog rin-po-che'i mdzod*, I, p. 535. See also *Tshig-don rin-po-che'i mdzod*, p. 59, 61, 139 ff. There are 'four' lamps, intricately interconnected, each of them indicating some deeper aspect of the process of experience.

24) *Theg-pa'i mchog rin-po-che'i mdzod*, I, p. 487. This hierarchical ordering indicates a gradation which in terms of 'realms' may be explained as the 'objective' realm including body, speech, and mind, as these can be investigated 'objectively'; the 'subjective' realm which is dealt with in terms of existentiality (the feeling and conviction of being a subject), communication (the feeling and conviction of having something to communicate which is different from the mere noise of talk), and spirituality (the feeling and conviction of being more than a rigid model turned myth); last, there is the 'totality' realm which is neither of the foregoing but comprises both. This triadic hierarchy has certain affinities with the triadic approach offered by Erich Jantsch, *Design for Evolution*, p. 92 and *passim*.

25) *Theg-pa'i mchog rin-po-che'i mdzod*, I, p. 491; see also pp. 496, 497. *Tshig-don rin-po-che'i mdzod*, p. 129.

26) Ibid.

27) *Theg-pa'i mchog rin-po-che'i mdzod*, II, p. 492 f.

28) *Theg-pa'i mchog rin-po-che'i mdzod*, I, p. 492; see also *Tshig-don rin-po-che'i mdzod*, p. 130.

29) *Theg-pa'i mchog rin-po-che'i mdzod*, I, p. 494.

30) Ibid.

31) *Theg-pa'i mchog rin-po-che'i mdzod*, I, pp. 502 f.

32) *Tshig-don rin-po-che'i mdzod*, p. 135; see also pp. 72 f. Another term for *rang-bzhin*, 'actuality' (which is, as it were, the link between the 'other side' and 'our side'), is *gnyis-med* 'non-duality', illustrated by the image of a mirror and the reflection of a face in it, sleep and dream, and a river and its waves, in *Lung-gi gter-mdzod*, 70a.

33) *mKha'-'gro snying-thig*, part 1, p. 61; *mKha'-'gro yang-thig*, part 2, p. 172. *Theg-pa mtha'-dag-gi gsal-bas byed-pa Grub-pa'i mtha rin-po-che'i mdzod*, p. 366. Inasmuch as, according to *Lung-gi gter-mdzod*, p. 104b, the 'conductors', 'motility', and 'bioenergetic input', belong to the realm of imagination which is the capacity to set up a mental image (*yid-kyi yul*), they are not absolute truths about human nature, nor are they ever meant to be absolute truths. Rather, they are a kind of 'hypothesis', put forth to explain what has been found to be invariant and to facilitate *further* probings which take place within the person himself. As a 'hypothesis' they have a good chance of being correct (functionally true, though not representationally true) in a domain that reaches beyond the ordinary level of the relatively invariant. On the significance of the search for invariance, see "Appendix: Physics and Perception," in David Bohm, *The Special Theory of Relativity*.

34) Briefly mentioned in *Theg-pa mtha'-dag-gi don gsal-bar byed-pa Grub-pa'i mtha' rin-po-che'i mdzod*, p. 367, and discussed in greater detail in *Tshig-don rin-po-che'i mdzod*, pp. 127 f, and *mKha'-'gro yang-thig*, part 3, pp. 119 f.

35) *mKha'-'gro yang-thig*, part 2, pp. 172 f. The quotation from the *Rig-pa rang-shar chen-po'i rgyud* does not seem to be in the text as found in *rNying-ma rgyud-'bum*, vol. 10; the quotation from the *Senge-ge rtsal-rdzogs chen-po'i rgyud* is found in *rNying-ma rgyud-'bum*, vol. 9, p. 247; *rNying-ma'i rgyud bcu-bdun*, vol. 2, p. 257.

36) This is the term for the decisive pattern in the 'other side' as discussed in *Tshig-don rin-po-che'i mdzod*, pp. 127 f.

37) *mKha'-'gro yang-thig*, part 2, pp. 154 f.

38) Ibid., p. 155.

39) Ibid.

40) *Theg-pa'i mchog rin-po-che'i mdzod*, II, p. 367.

41) *Lung-gi gter-mdzod*, pp. 104a ff.

42) See *rNying-ma rgyud-'bum*, vol. 10, p. 514.

43) Ibid.

Notes to Chapter One

1) *Theg-pa chen-po'i man-ngag-gi bstan-bcos Yid-bzhin rin-po-che'i mdzod*, p. 78; and its commentary, *Padma dkar-po*, pp. 827 f. It is important to note that Klong-chen rab-'byams-pa considers this practice to be preliminary to *bsam-gtan*.

2) *sngags* (*gsang-sngags*). See *Kindly Bent to Ease Us*, part 1, p. 289 n.22.

3) *Theg-pa chen-po'i man-ngag-gi bstan-bcos Yid-bzhin rin-po-che'i mdzod*, p. 78, and its commentary, *Padma dkar-po*, p. 828.

4) *Padma dkar-po*, p. 828.

5) *gzugs-sku* and *chos-sku*. On these terms see *Kindly Bent to Ease Us*, part 1, pp. 268 n.18, 276 n.10, and p. 223 in particular.

6) *dpal kun-tu bzang-po-la phyag-'tshal-lo*. The invocation is the same as in *Kindly Bent to Ease Us*, part 1. See p. 250 n.1 for Klong-chen rab-'byams-pa's interpretation of it in the context of that work.

   Inasmuch as *bsam-gtan* involves the whole of man in his self-development, the invocation is explained by Klong-chen rab-'byams-pa in his *Ngal-gso skor-gsum-gyi spyi-don legs-bshad rgya-mtsho*, pp. 108 f, as implying the following in the process of starting-point ⟶ path ⟶ goal:

   > As for the starting-point, *dpal* means self-existent pristine cognitiveness. *kun-tu* means the (Buddha) intentionality in which the founding strata of meaning and their founded pristine cognitions are such that they cannot be added to nor

subtracted from each other insofar as their intentionality, throughout the three aspects of time, does not step out of itself nor turn into something other than itself; and *bzang-po* means not to stir away from it. *phyag-'tshal-lo* ('Praise to') means to understand their value.

As for the path, *dpal* means the (Buddha) intentionality as the founding stratum of meaning in which pure awareness, the mind as limpid clearness and consummate perspicacity, is comfortably settled. *kun-tu* means for all eternity not to abandon its reach and range. *bzang-po* means that, if we do not abandon the reach and range of the founding stratum of meaning, the whole of 'appearance' and of 'mind' comes as an (amusing) play that takes place in original freedom and absolute completeness. *phyag-'tshal-lo* means to make efforts to make one's creative imagination reach the center of meaningfulness.

As for the goal, *dpal* means the primordial Lord who, having come as the (spiritual) teacher for Saṃsāra and Nirvāṇa, resides as the indissoluble unity of founding stratum and founded pristine cognitions in the secret chamber of our precious existence. *kun-tu* means to reveal the pure realm of 'Og-min with its five certainties, and *bzang-po* means to train the six kinds of sentient beings in their respective stations in life through the play-like manifestation of (individual) Buddhas, by means of 'great Compassion' that issues from this realm. *phyag-'tshal-lo* means to present our offerings joyfully and devotedly.

On the 'primordial Lord' see *Kindly Bent to Ease Us*, part 1, p. 250 n.2. 'Og-min may be rendered freely as 'spiritual realm', whose many facets are ways of understanding. A lengthy discussion is found in Klong-chen rab-'byams-pa's *dPal gsang-ba'i snying-po de-kho-na-nyid nges-pa'i rgyud-kyi 'grel-pa phyogs-bcu'i mun-pa thams-cad rnam-par sel-ba*, fol. 21a ff.

7) *rgyal-'gong*, name for a male mischievous spirit.

8) *bsen-mo*, name for a female spirit.

9) *mkha'-'gro*, also *mkha'-'gro-ma*, are positive in nature; *ma-mo* are negative.

10) *the'u rangs*, name for a male mischievous spirit.

11) *gsal-dangs.* There is a subtle difference between these two terms. *gsal* implies emission or seeming emission of light, an effulgence which, in a sense, is transfigured by light. *dangs* does not emit any light.

12) *bdud.* In his *Lung-gi gter-mdzod*, fol. 170ab, Klong-chen rab-'byams-pa gives a short, but very lucid, explanation of this term. 'Spiritual death' is our dichotomic way of thinking. A detailed analysis is given by dPal-sprul O-rgyan 'Jigs-med chos-kyi dbang-po in his *bDud-kyi rgyu brtags-te spong-tshul-gyi man-ngag bdud-las rnam-rgyal* (in Collected Works, vol. 2, pp. 639–73).

Notes to Chapter Two

1) *Shing-rta rnam-par dag-pa*, p. 50.

2) It is unfortunate that both the Tibetan term *bla-ma* and the Sanskrit word *guru* have been horribly misused, be it out of ignorance or out of self-aggrandisement.

Padma-phrin-las-snying-po in his *Bla-med nang rgyud-sde-gsum-gyi rgyal-chos padma'i zhal-gdams lam-rim ye-snying 'grel-pa ye-shes brjed-byang gcig-bsdus ye-shes lam-'jug*, p. 429, explains:

The word *bla-ma* stands for the Sanskrit word *guru* which has the two meanings of 'weighty' (heavy) and 'light' (ethereal). As there is an abundance of capabilities there is weightiness, and as there is no limitation by evil there is lightness. This meaning also applies to primordial pristine cognitiveness: 'weightiness' by virtue of capabilities because all the capabilities that constitute Buddhahood are present in completeness; and 'lightness' by virtue of the absence of defects because one's being has never been experienced as defiled by the incidental impurity that is this paradox of there being a presence where there is nothing.

From the rNying-ma Tantras we learn that *bla-ma* is the totality field of experience that has as its 'cause' (the 'triggering' of) the presence in Mind-as-such (*sems-nyid rgyu'i bla-ma*) and finds its 'goal' (the culmination of the process) in our individual minds when operating as pristine cognitions (*'bras-bu sems-kyi bla-ma, 'bras-bu ye-shes bla-ma*) in its 'framework of meanings as a presence' (*snang-ba chos-kyi bla-ma, snang-ba chos-nyid bla-ma*). See *Byang-sems man-ngag-rin-chen phreng-ba* (subtitle *Bang-mdzod 'phrul-gyi lde-mig*) (in *rNying-ma rgyud-'bum*, vol. 2, pp. 149–208), p. 154; *rDzogs-pa chen-po nges-don 'dus-pa'i rgyud lta-ba thams-cad-kyi snying-po rin-po-che rnam-par bkod-pa* (Ibid., vol. 7, pp. 124–478), pp. 221 f. The various facets of experience as nine *bla-ma* are discussed in the *sNang-srid kha-sbyor bdud-rtsi bcud-thig-'khor-ba thog-mtha' gcod-pa'i rgyud* (Ibid., vol. 5, pp. 525–601), p. 599. On the subtle distinction between *sems-nyid* and *sems*, see *Kindly Bent to Ease Us*, part 1.

3) *Shing-rta rnam-par dag-pa*, p. 52.

4) As Klong-chen rab-'byams-pa concisely states in his *Theg-pa mtha'-dag-gi don gsal-bar byed-pa Grub-pa'i mtha' rin-po-che'i mdzod*, p. 178, the *prātimokṣa* comprises five kinds of persons who have already renounced or are about to renounce the world, as well as two kinds who continue to live the life of a householder. The former are a fully ordained monk or nun, a novice, male or female, having taken the vow of renunciation but not yet admitted into the order, and a person preparing himself for being admitted into the higher order; the latter are lay de-votees, male and female. What distinguishes those covered by the *prātimokṣa* from ordinary persons is that they impose upon themselves a discipline whereby they will eventually be able to follow the path.

5) *Shing-rta rnams-par dag-pa*, p. 53.

6) 'Confidence' (*dad-pa*) is a summary term for a number of states of mind aiding a person's spiritual growth. Traditionally, three kinds are distinguished. See H. V. Guenther & Leslie S. Kawamura, *Mind in Buddhist Psychology*, p. 39. However, Klong-chen rab-'byams-pa in his *Theg-pa chen-po'i man-ngag-gyi bstan-bcos Yid-bzhin rin-po-che'i mdzod*, pp. 62–65, and his com-mentary on it, the *Padma dkar-po*, pp. 744–62, distinguishes six kinds and arranges them as follows: "eagerness, curiosity, ded-ication, clarity, trust, and pursuit of one's objective with cer-

tainty and in certitude." Of them, curiosity, dedication, and clarity fall under 'lucid confidence' in the traditional scheme, interest and trust under 'trusting confidence', and the pursuit of one's objective with certainty and in certitude is the very implementation of 'longing confidence' or eagerness in Klong-chen rab-'byams-pa's redefinition. Thus he says:

> Eagerness makes a person accept or reject according to the
>   relationship that exists between cause and effect;
> Curiosity makes a mind apply itself to the most high;
> Dedication makes a person most conscientious;
> Clarity lets virtue shine brightly in the mind;
> Trust abolishes doubt about the real meaning of life;
> And pursuit of one's objective with certainty and in
>   certitude is to have supreme confidence in the
>   most high,
> As it emerges when one listens to (its exposition), ponders
>   (its meaning), and brings it to life in one's own being.

Klong-chen rab-'byams-pa then discusses each kind of confidence as to its nature, definition, subdivision, appropriate illustration, and indication of its presence in an individual. Once confidence is present in a person, it does the following for him:

> Confidence is like the fertile soil.
> As the foundation of all that is, it increases the amount of
>   what is wholesome and healthy.
> It is like a boat crossing the river of fictitious being.
> It is like an escort protecting against (spiritual) death and
>   emotional assault.
> It is like a carriage travelling to the island of freedom.
> It is like the king of all jewels, making whatever one
>   intends to come true.
> It is like a hero, crushing evil.
> It is the most precious hoard amongst the worthwhile
>   accumulations.

But where there is no confidence, there is no chance whatsoever to grow and to escape from one's self-imposed limitations:

In those who have no chance (to win freedom), there is no
confidence whatsoever.
Deficiency in confidence knows no bounds.
It is like the bottomless boundless sea: nowhere can the
dry land of freedom be found.
It is like a ship without a steersman, which will never set
(its passengers) free from fictitious being.
It is like a person with maimed hands who has arrived (at
the land of gold), but has no chance to clothe himself in
what is wholesome and healthy.
It is like a burnt seed, which will not grow the sprout of
limpid clearness and consummate perspicacity.
It is like a blind person, for whom there is no light to see.
It is like someone who has been thrown into the dungeon
of Saṃsāra, and can but move about in Saṃsāra.

Klong-chen rab-'byams-pa then goes on to discuss the ways
and means of generating confidence and making it gain in
strength, as well as the circumstances under which it may
wane.

7) In his *Shing-rta rnam-par dag-pa*, p. 50, Klong-chen rab-
'byams-pa likens perseverance and the desire to escape from
one's present situation to the soil; the feeling of disgust with
one's situation to the going out into the field; the concern with
liberation to the seed to be planted which eventually will grow
into the desired fruit of limpid clearness and consummate
perspicacity; the dismissing of thoughts concerned with this
life only to the field work; and the looking forward to the
harvest—the tending of the inner capabilities—to manure.

8) The basic text, as well as its reproduction in *Shing-rta rnam-par
dag-pa* have *bstan* 'teaching' instead of *brtan* 'firmness'. But in
his explanation on p. 50, Klong-chen rab-'byams-pa makes no
reference to 'teaching', but speaks of 'a firm mind' (*blo-brtan*).

9) In *Shing-rta rnam-par dag-pa*, p. 52, Klong-chen rab-'byams-pa
states that the Śrāvaka abides by the rules of the *prātimokṣa* in
order to find his answer to life's problems. The Bodhisattva,
that is, ethical man, extends his search for life's meaning over

three 'countless aeons', which is to say that while the Śrāvaka acts on the egoistic principle, ethical man acts on the benevolent principle. The mystic attempts to find the answer in his lifetime by the realization that these two principles operate in a wider field, and it is this field that is of sole importance.

10) That the three obligations belong to one and the same person is the theme of mNga'-ris paṇḍita Padma dbang-gyi rgyal-po's (1487–1542) *Rang-bzhin rdzogs-pa chen-po'i lam-gyi cha-lag sdom-pa gsum rnam-par nges-pa*, to which Lo-chen Dharma-śrī (1654–1717) of sMin-grol-gling wrote the famous commentary, *sDom-gsum 'grel-pa legs-bshad ngo-mtshan dpag-bsam-gyi ste-mo*. The *sDom-gsum rnam-par nges-pa'i mchan-'grel rig-pa 'dzin-pa'i 'jugs-mgogs*, by a certain Gu-ṇa (on p. 279), quotes Klong-chen rab-'byams-pa's words.

11) In his *Theg-pa mtha'-dag-gi gsal-bar byed-pa Grub-pa'i mtha' rin-po-che'i mdzod*, p. 188, Klong-chen rab-'byams-pa elaborates on *Mahāyānottaratantraśāstra*, I, 157, in which it is plainly stated that self-denigration is an impediment to spiritual growth.

NOTES TO CHAPTER THREE

1) *Theg-pa chen-po'i man-ngag-gi bstan-bcos Yid-bzhin rin-po-che'i mdzod*, p. 78, and its commentary, *Padma dkar-po*, p. 829, where Klong-chen rab-'byams-pa adds: "In the same way as a sprout grows due to many causes and conditions, so also the growth of this pristine cognitiveness will not come about just because it exists within us, but it needs many actions (appropriate to its growth)." It is scarcely necessary to emphasize that *thabs* never means 'random activity'.

2) *Shing-rta rnam-par dag-pa*, pp. 74 f: "The meaning of the word (*dbang* derives from) *abhiṣiñca* and *ṣikata* (*sic!*), to wash off dirt and to assign a certain portion. Further, one speaks of empowerment because of the power to link up with the vision of truth on the first spiritual level, in this one's lifetime."
   In the *Khyad-par chos-spyod-kyi khrid-rim lam-rim 'od-kyi phreng-ba* (in *Bla-ma dgongs-pa 'dus-pa*, vol. 5 [in *Ngagyur Nyingmay*

Sungrab, vol. 48]), pp. 55 f., three etymologies are offered. The one which is derived from *abhiṣiñca* is connected with 'cleansing', "in the same way as a vessel that has been thoroughly cleansed is fit to have liquids poured into it." The one derived from *abhiṣikata* (*sic*!) is connected with 'assigning a portion', "in the same way as a father gives an allowance to his son." The one derived from *abhisiti* (*sic*!) is connected with 'maturation' "in the same way as a king makes his ministers and subjects accept his orders."

There is quite a variety of rituals that go with what is implied by the term *dbang*, and this has the effect that the names for these 'empowerments' may be similar in the context in which they occur, but their content is quite different in each case. This is clearly stated by Yon-tan rgya-mtsho in his *Zab-don snang-byed nyi-ma'i 'od-zer*, p. 100.

In rDzogs-chen practice the *dbang* refers to intrapsychic processes.

Lastly, the order of these empowerments involves a hierarchy in the 'founding' (*rten*) and the 'founded' (*brten*) which on the surface is the body-mind complex.

3) This is clearly stated by Yon-tan rgya-mtsho in his *Zab-don snang-byed nyi-ma'i 'od-zer*, pp. 185, 190, 192.

4) In his *Theg-pa mtha'-dag-gi don gsal-bar byed-pa Grub-pa'i mtha' rin-po-che'i mdzod*, p. 372, Klong-chen rab-'byams-pa even goes so far as to state:

> Although it has been said that attention to and cultivation of the Developing and Fulfillment Stages are of primary importance on the ordinary way of self-growth, they have to be dismissed because they do not lead beyond subjective speculation. But on this uncommon way here, the pristine cognitiveness that is sheer lucency is seen directly, beyond all subjective operations concerning mental constructs.

He goes on to stress the point that the real aim of 'meditation' is to become free from the restrictive operations of the mind, the noetic-noematic complex which cannot but operate within its limitations, and to make the 'jump' to 'pristine cognitiveness' which is inclusive as it involves a whole world-outlook.

5) This variety of terms reflects the difficulty of trying to name or talk about the totality field of experience, because it is impossible to make ostensive definitions. Primarily, these terms indicate the shift of viewpoint which has carried with it freedom from old concerns and a wider vision and perspective that has been so startling that it has to be talked about. Maybe the most difficult terms are *rig-pa* and *lhan-cig-skyes-pa*. The former, although for want of a better term rendered as 'pure awareness', is far from implying anything static or merely receptive. It is 'informative' without having recourse to concepts, and it is 'ecstatic' in being the highest form of pleasurable excitement when the currents (*rlung*, 'motility') are so strong that the person has the feeling of being 'lit up', 'radiating light' (*gsal-ba*) like a star, which is due to the bioenergetic input flowing at its optimum capacity. The latter (*lhan-cig-skyes-pa*) indicates that the totality field of experience is always with us in its totality and completeness, and insofar as it is so, it is a 'setting' (*bsam-gtan*). Most of the terms occur together in Klong-chen rab-'byams-pa's *Theg-pa chen-po'i man-ngag-gi bstan-bcos Yid-bzhin rin-po-che'i mdzod*, pp. 79ff, and he explains them in the *Padma dkar-po*, pp. 939 f:

> The pristine cognitiveness in wider perspective, having
>   come about through the above technique, is such that
> In its reach and range of radiance and pleasure there is
>   nothing about it of presence or non-presence;
> The inner glow, passing beyond words that have to do
>   with such indices as that it is something existing or not
>   existing or that it is this or is not this, is
> A pure awareness, defying all propositions, shining in
>   pellucidity and radiance;
> It is like the orbs of sun and moon, steady in their
>   pellucidity and radiance
> In the range that is not broken up and has no sectors, like
>   the sky.
> Free from the mire of divisive concepts, it is like the ocean.
> In this self-existent pristine cognitiveness, Mind-as-such,
>   sheer lucency,
> Always attend to and bring to life that which is with and
>   in you,

The founding stratum of meaning, directly encountered by
  worthy persons.

In his commentary on this part, Klong-chen rab-'byams-pa
gives a very personal account by referring to the words of his
teacher and by stating that he found his own experiences
supported by the texts:

> In this state where, when I attended to motility, the pure
> awareness in its radiance was without concepts, and when I
> attended to the bioenergetic input, the pure awareness in its
> pleasure was radiant, I looked intently at this pure aware-
> ness in myself. Even in this barest (experience of) pleasure,
> radiance, and non-dividedness (by concepts), there was
> nothing of presence or non-presence. In the pure facticity of
> the pure awareness within me, radiant and open, there was
> nothing of it being this or not being this or of existing or not
> existing. This pure awareness, in which its very value of
> being beyond words and thought, indescribable by anal-
> ogies, has disappeared, was like an ocean, pellucid and
> steady; it was like the orbs of sun and moon, having no ideas
> about themselves in their radiance; it was like the wider
> expanse of the sky, unbroken and not falling into partiality.
> This pure awareness in each of us, in which the agitation of
> mind and mental events has subsided, is encountered as the
> founding stratum of meaning, Mahāmudrā, self-existent
> pristine cognitiveness, and it is said to be rDzogs-pa chen-
> po, Mādhyamika, the essence of the six topics of (Nāropa's)
> techniques, the very nature of the Path-and-the-Goal, the
> Zhi-byed (system) by which all agitatedness subsides, the
> Prajñāpāramitā dealing with the meaning of the experience
> of Being.

The freedom that comes with the shift of perspective is well
described in the subsequent verse:

> Whatever concepts with their ostensible designations
>   may arise
> Do so freely in this reach and range of the experience of
>   Being, like the waves in a river.
> It is important not to let slip this pellucidity in its relaxed
>   state.

Klong-chen rab-'byams-pa explains this verse to mean:

> When one attends to this state that is like the ocean, deep, calm, with no expanding and no contracting, there may arise concepts trying to move to the object; do not run after them so as to capture them rising, do not repress their being; when they have subsided by themselves and there is relaxation, do not let slip this pellucidity that has come through previous attention to it. Concepts are like waves, they will subside by themselves in the reach and range of sheer lucency. Because they have come from Mind-as-such and will untangle themselves in it, they are no different from it.

He then goes on to describe that which will lead to 'higher cognitions':

> Attend to self-existent pristine cognitiveness that is
>   with you,
> (In which) value-cognition is an incessant stream because
>   (its) setting has become pellucid,
> There occurring no depression, no gloominess, no elation,
> No attachment, no striving, free from every movement.
> This is the instruction in the most profound.

He explains this passage to imply the following:

> Whenever one engages in contemplative attention when either motility or the bioenergetic input level or the pure awareness is happily settled in itself, one has to attend in such a way that the cognitive capacity does not become depressed or gloomy, that dividing concepts do not rush forth, that one does not become attached to the sensations in this contemplation, that one does not move away from this state, that the circulation of breath is not felt, and that the separation of pellucidity from radiance is not vitiated by the intrusion of dividing concepts. That is to say, selective and discursive thinking, attachment to the feelings of joy and pleasure, and attention to respiratory movements are defects of the contemplative setting. Since breathing is a rushing forth, it is the vehicle of dividing concepts and is hence declared to be a defect. Thus, when one is in this range that is radiant from deep within, value-cognitions

proceed in an uninterrupted stream because they are inseparable from that appreciative cognition that is a self-existent sheer lucency. This one has to attend to constantly.

From all this we can gather that the transition must come freely and that it cannot be forced. Hence, the reference to breathing does not mean to stop breathing or to hold one's breath for a period of time, but ordinary 'shallow' breathing as the vehicle for the rush of concepts must change over into a different rhythm. The reference to selective and discursive thinking and what follows is a description of the phases of 'meditation' (*dhyāna*) found in the canonical texts. This kind of 'meditation' which remains within the subject-object dichotomy, is quite different from 'rDzogs-chen meditation'. Unfortunately, the same term (*bsam-gtan*) is used for both forms.

6) *Shing-rta rnam-par dag-pa*, p. 81. 'Non-dividedness' (*mi-rtog-pa*) is a short-hand term for a process that can be paraphrased only at some length. *rtog-pa* indicates the first step in the direction of conceptualization (*rnam-par rtog-pa*) by introducing a split in the continuum of experience as a dynamic field. The field itself has no 'split' (*rtog-med*). Therefore, *mi-rtog-pa* suggests non-interference with the continuum. Interference (*rtog-pa*) is to divide unity into a curiously mosaic pattern in which each configurative element is taken separately.

7) This 'thrust towards Being' (*de-bzhin gshegs-pa'i snying-po* in the parlance of speculative-philosophical works, and *bde-bar gshegs-pa'i snying-po* in that of the 'existential' approach to man's problem) is referred to by two other terms as long as it operates in a living being. The one, *rigs*, indicates the 'affinity with Being' which takes on various forms individually; the other, *khams*, indicates the 'bioenergetic level' and is basically operational. As such, these terms specifically indicate the quality of either an ordinary sentient person or a more advanced person such as 'ethical man'. They are used figuratively only with respect to someone who has reached the Buddha-level. Klong-chen rab-'byams-pa discusses this problem most lucidly in his *Theg-pa mtha'-dag-gi don gsal-bar byed-pa Grub-pa'i mtha' rin-po-che'i mdzod*, pp. 167, 173, 183.

8) *gzhi'i rgyud.* This term refers to the primacy of Being, of which both an ordinary sentient being and a Buddha is an 'explication'. Being as a continuum is implied by the use of this term *rgyud* with reference to either 'explication'. Being-(as-such) therefore reverberates in the concrete being of an individual as he understands (or fails to understand) himself. See *Theg-pa'i mchog rin-po-che'i mdzod,* I, p. 177. As Klong-chen rab-'byams-pa concisely states in his *Theg-pa mtha'-dag-gi don gsal-bar byed-pa Grub-pa'i mtha' rin-po-che'i mdzod,* p. 386, this *gzhi'i rgyud* is 'self-existent pristine cognitiveness'.

9) *Theg-pa'i mchog rin-po-che'i mdzod,* I, pp. 547 f.

In his *mKha'-'gro yan-tig,* part 2, p. 161, Klong-chen rab-'byams-pa explains the term *ye-shes-kyi rlung* ('motility as the carrier of pristine cognitiveness') as follows:

> *ye-shes-kyi rlung* is the name of pure awareness that comes from 'responsiveness' (in the triadic pattern of Being). Since this triad of facticity, actuality, and responsiveness is indivisible, it is (for this reason that it is operationally) termed 'pristine cognitiveness'. Since in its mere stirring, in its mere flashing, it is similar to the breeze of the wind, it is called 'motility'. Motility in the concrete refers to the emergence of the noetic-noematic complex which is its pathway. The effulgence of pristine cognitiveness as a mere flash is carried away by the horse of motility and becomes the many consciousness-patterns. The *ye-shes-kyi rlung* is, in its facticity, an utter openness and hence defies any limitations by propositions; as to actuality, it is radiance and hence manifests itself as founding stratum and founded pristine cognitions; as to responsiveness, it is pure awareness and hence arises as a pristine cognitiveness that is an overall sensitivity and a pristine cognitiveness that is sensitive to detailed observable qualities.

He then goes on to criticize severely those who do not understand that 'motility' has quite different connotations in different situations because there is a great difference between 'pristine cognitiveness' (*ye-shes*) and the 'noetic-noematic complex' (*sems*), engrossed in its constructs that lead to karmic consequences.

10) The Developing Stage and the Fulfillment Stage, which must enter the unity of experience, rather than remain separate exercises.

11) According to Klong-chen rab-'byams-pa's *Zab-mo yang-tig*, part 1, pp. 193 f, the following refers to specific methods of reinstating the state of non-dividedness, aided by attention to 'motility', the energetic currents (*rlung*) as they flow along the 'conductors' (*rtsa*), and to the 'bioenergetic input' (*thig-le*) which is felt to be pervasive of the whole organism.

12) *bdud-rtsi*. 'Nectar' is the term found in dictionaries which offer little help when one deals with technical matters. In rDzogs-chen thought *bdud-rtsi* refers to a process of transformation or transfiguration. The word is analyzed into its components *bdud*, used to cover all that we could term 'constructs of the mind, 'the darkness that comes with a decline in pure awareness', 'the straying into the triple world', 'the poison of emotions', 'the mind in its state of roaming in the triple world', 'the sentient being in Saṃsāra', and so on, and *rtsi*, used to indicate the opposites such as 'founding stratum of meaning in which no dividing concepts occur', 'absolute pristine cognitiveness', 'the return from having strayed into Saṃsāra', and so on. See *sNang-srid-kha-sbyor bdud-rtsi bcud-thig 'khor-ba thog-mtha' gcod-pa'i rgyud phyi-ma* (in *rNying-ma rgyud-'bum*, vol. 6, pp. 1–52), pp. 3 ff.

   Ngag-dbang bstan-'dzin rdo-rje, in his *Klong-chen snying-gi thig-le'i mkha'-'gro bde-chen rgyal-mo'i sgrub-gzhung-gi 'grel-pa rgyud-don snang-ba*, pp. 30 f, quotes from the *bDud-rtsi sgron-gsal* to the effect that "Saṃsāra, resembling *bdud* (Māra, the personification of spiritual death), is painted (*rtsi btang*) with absolute pristine cognitiveness, and hence one speaks of *bdud-rtsi*." He goes on to give further examples of these hermeneutical interpretations which are based on certain experiences.

   The title of the work from which Ngag-dbang bstan-'dzin rdo-rje quotes occurs as a chapter title in *sNang-srid kha-sbyor bdud-rtsi bcud-thig 'khor-ba thog-mtha' gcod-pa'i rgyud* (in *rNying-ma rgyud-'bum*, vol. 5, pp. 526–601), p. 553, but this passage is not found there, but occurs in the *bDud-rtsi rin-po-che ye-shes gsang-ba'i 'khor-lo'i rgyud* (in *rNying-ma rgyud-'bum*, vol. 26, pp. 1–58), pp. 8 f.

13) In the basic text Klong-chen rab-'byams-pa speaks of 'pellucidity' (*dvangs*), but in the commentary the term *rang-bzhin*, as such', 'as it actually is there', is used.

14) The sky (*nam-mkha'*) is used here as a symbol for unlimited expansion which is hierarchically ordered. To the extent that ('objectively') the external reference is lost and gives way to an utter openness that is yet radiant in its immediately felt presence (*stong-gsal phyi'i nam-mkha'*), there is internally ('subjectively') a vastness that is not limited by dividing concepts (*rtod-med nang-gi nam-mkha'*), and this merges in a totality field and is understood as pure (naked) cognitiveness that is 'informative' (*rig*) and an utter openness (*stong*). *Shing-rta rnam-par dag-pa*, p. 90.

15) The five emotions: desire-attachment, irritation-aversion, dullness-lusterlessness, arrogance (ego inflation) and envy-jealousy. These emotions form part and parcel of the noetic-noematic complex (*sems*). Their presence in a person's mind is beautifully illustrated in the *rDzogs-pa chen-po kun-tu bzang-po'i dgongs-pa zang-thal-gyi rgyud-chen mthong-ba dang thos-pa dang smon-lam btab-pa tsam-gyis sangs-rgya-ba'i rgyud* (in *rDzogs-pa chen-po dgongs-pa zang-thal*, vol. 4, pp. 81–181), p. 117:

> When irritation-aversion is born in the mind, it is like the start of fierce, wild winter storms; when desire-attachment is born it is like water rushing downhill; when dullness-lusterlessness is born it is like fog thickening; when arrogance is born it is like the wind fighting with rocks; and when envy-jealousy is born it is like water rushing down a ravine.

16) In his *Shing-rta rnam-par dag-pa*, pp. 93 f, Klong-chen rab-'byams-pa illustrates each of the three indicators (pleasure, radiance, non-dividedness) in their 'entropic' character, by ten instances, five of which tend to make each indicator an end in itself and to have it pursued purely 'subjectively' as if it could be 'possessed', so that the person pursuing it is 'obsessed with' it. Five other instances are the obverse of the above overevaluations.

17) In his *Shing-rta rnam-par dag-pa*, pp. 94 f, Klong-chen rab-'byams-pa states that it is easy to mend any deficiency by its appropriate counteragent, but it remains a sort of patch-work. Most important is to go to the very root whence the deficiency has started, that is, to realize that whatever there is, positive or negative, is the play of 'pure awareness' (*rig-pa*), the ultimate source of our being, which in its play is 'positive' when we go along with it, but 'negative' when we try to go against it.

18) As Klong-chen rab-'byams-pa states in his *Shing-rta rnam-par dag-pa*, p. 98, this is the theme of the third part of his trilogy and is detailed in the commentary on it.

19) *rdo-rje'i bum-pa* is a term referring to the 'energy body' (*rdo-rje'i lus*). The syllabic sound symbol HŪM connects this 'reservoir' with the central 'conductor' which, in turn, is a 'link' with the totality of Being.

20) This refers to the 'foundation' for living beings, as it evolved in the self-evolution of the cosmos. It had its origin through the cosmic 'wind' that caused clouds to gather and to pour down their rain forming an ocean on which the 'earth' came into existence. See *Padma dkar-po*, p. 45.

21) A Tantra belonging to the Kriyā division. It is the basic Tantra in the Japanese Shingon sect.

22) In his *Shing-rta rnam-par dag-pa*, p. 107, Klong-chen rab-'byams-pa, in support of this statement, quotes from the *sGyu-'phrul dra-ba*. But his quotation is not in the Tantra that goes by this name. The translation of the various ingredients is only tentative. The specific connotations of the general terms vary from district to district.

23) It is at this stage that a process can be initiated that has most often been misunderstood. In his *Shing-rta rnam-par dag-pa* pp. 108 f, Klong-chen rab-'byams-pa distinguishes between *phyag-rgya(-ma)* and *rig-ma*, where he defines the latter as *yid-gi rig-ma*, thus emphasizing that the process described in the following passage, in spite of its ostensible sexual character,

actually is a psychic (imaginative) process that owes much to 'internalization'. The motions that are described indicate that the whole person is actively engaged in the revitalization by a seemingly sexual excitation. In his *Theg-pa'i mchog rin-po-che'i mdzod*, I, p. 301, Klong-chen rab-'byams-pa states that *rig-ma* means the following:

> *rig-pa* is so called because the pristine cognition that comes from pure awareness is known directly, and *ma* means that since there is nobody in the world who does not depend on a mother (*ma*), there is no emergence of Buddhahood without its dependence on a *rig-ma* who is like the earth.

And on p. 302 he explains *phyag-rgya-ma* as follows:

> *phyag* is 'to hold', that is, to hold (a person) away from Saṃsāra and on to the level of Buddhahood. *rgya* is 'to seal', that is, to seal Saṃsāra with limpid clearness and consummate perspicacity; *ma* means that this is similar to vital food. In the same way as there is death when there is no food, so there cannot come any understanding (of Being) without its dependence on a *phyag-rgya-ma*, and when this understanding does not come, there is bondage in the triple world.

It seems that, at Klong-chen rab-'byams-pa's time, misunderstanding of what was actually involved was as rampant as it is still today in the Western world which has the added disadvantage of being caught in the 'literalist's' fallacy whenever non-Western source material is involved. Again and again, throughout his works, Klong-chen rab-'byams-pa emphasizes the distinctness of the rDzogs-chen approach to life's meaning from the other techniques, and there is a veiled contempt for those of 'low intelligence'. See *Lung-gi gter-mdzod*, 105a ff; *Tshig-don rin-po-che'i mdzod*, pp. 134 ff.

There are essentially two attitudes involved, the one is concerned with the 'what' and hence emphasizes 'techniques' to such a degree that everything else is intentionally ignored. This is the obsession with sex, to give only one example, and it figures predominantly in the realm of the *thabs-lam* ('procedure by techniques'). The other is the attitude of him who 'stands above' and is concerned with the 'how'. This is the *grol-lam* ('procedure in and through freedom'). Klong-chen rab-'byams-pa is a representative of the *grol-lam*.

24) In his *Shing-rta rnam-par dag-pa*, p. 112, Klong-chen rab-'byams-pa adds that the important point is to know what it is all about, and that to go through such motions as detailed above in a repeat performance is of no avail, but rather a path on which all one's efforts are merely wasted away.

25) As Klong-chen rab-'byams-pa in his *Shing-rta rnam-par dag-pa*, p. 113, clearly states, these techniques never go beyond the subjective level concerned with its objective reference, thus maintaining the dividedness that is to be overcome.

26) The Zhi-byed system goes back to the teaching of the Indian master Dam-pa sangs-rgyas, a pupil of Maitripa. In Tibet Dam-pa sangs-rgyas became the teacher of the remarkable woman Ma-gcig lab-sgron-ma (1055–1145) whose gCod system is still alive today. Mahāmudrā is the leitmotif of the teachings of the Indian Mahāsiddhas and was developed in Tibet by the bKa'-brgyud-pa school. Prajñāpāramitā, "the method to reach the other shore by the development of discriminative appreciation," and Mādhyamika, "pursuing a middle course," refer to the traditional epistemological and argumentative approaches respectively.

Selected
Bibliography*

Collections

Bla-ma dgongs-'dus. A Cycle of Precious Teachings and Practices of the Nyingma Tradition Rediscovered from its Place of Concealment by gTer-chen Sangs-rgyas gling-pa (in *Ngagyur Nyingmay Sungrab Series*, vols. 44–56). Gangtok, 1972.

Works in Western Languages

Bohm, David. *The Special Theory of Relativity.* New York: Benjamin, 1965.

Guenther, Herbert V. & Leslie S. Kawamura. *Mind in Buddhist Psychology.* Emeryville, Ca.: Dharma Publishing, 1975.

Jantsch, Erich. *Design for Evolution.* New York: Braziller, 1975.

Individual Tibetan Works

Gu-ṇa:
sDom-gsum rnam-par nges-pa'i mchan-'grel rig-pa 'dzin-pa'i 'jug-ngogs.

---

*Supplemental to Part One

Ngag-dbang bstan-'dzin rdo-rje:

Klong-chen snying-gi thig-le'i mkha'-'gro bde-chen rgyal-mo'i sgrub-gzhung-gi 'grel-pa rgyud-don snang-ba (in *Ngagyur Nyingmay Sungrab Series*, vol. 28). New Delhi, 1972.

Padma-phrin-las-snying-po:

Bla-med nang rgyud-sde-gsum-gyi rgyal-chos padma'i zhal-gdams lam-rim ye-snying 'grel-pa ye-shes brjed-byang gcig-bsdus ye-shes lam-'jug (in *Smanrtsis Shesrig Spendzod*, vol. 8). Leh, 1971.

Padma dbang-gi rgyal-po (mNga'-ris paṇḍita):

Rang-bzhin rdzogs-pa chen-po'i lam-gyi cha-lag sdom-pa gsum rnam-par nges-pa. Kalimpong, n.d.

dPal-sprul O-rgyan 'Jigs-med chos-kyi dbang-po:

bDud-kyi rgyu brtags-te spong-tshul-gyi man-ngag bdud-las rnam-rgyal (The Collected Works of —, vol. 2, pp. 639–73, in *Ngagyur Nyingmay Sungrab Series*, vol. 39).

Index

TECHNICAL TERMS

Tibetan

Sanskrit

Names and Subjects